It Takes a Church to Raise a Christian

It Takes a Church to Raise a Christian

How the Community of God Transforms Lives

Tod E. Bolsinger

Published by Brazos Press
a division of Baker Book House Company
P.O. Box 6287, Grand Rapids, MI 49516-6287
www.brazospress.com

Printed in the United States of America

Library of Congress Cataloging-in-Publication Data
Bolsinger, Tod E.
It takes a church to raise a Christian : how the community of God transforms lives / Tod E. Bolsinger.
p. cm.
Revision of the author's thesis (doctoral)—Fuller Theological Seminary, 1991.
ISBN 1-58743-089-4 (pbk.)
1. Spiritual life—Christianity. 2. Spiritual formation. I. Title.
BV4501.3.B655 2004
248.2—dc22 2003018979

Contents

For Beth . . . for everything

Acknowledgments

This book began as a Ph.D. dissertation at Fuller Theological Seminary in 1991. Now, as I offer it in a revised form to the greater community of Christ, it seems fitting that I acknowledge the way my communities have shaped my life, ministry, and writing for more than a decade. Like our Triune God who, while indivisible, is often considered both in the individual persons and one substance, I feel compelled to give thanks publicly to both individual people and the *essence* of their care for me simultaneously.

Fuller Theological Seminary not only taught me, but formed me. While I was mentored by Robert Banks and Ray Anderson, I sat under and learned from virtually the entire theology faculty at one time or another. Now when I have opportunities to teach for Fuller as an adjunct professor, the students continue to serve me through their thoughtful interaction with this material and their dedication to building faithful communities of God's transforming power.

I must express thanks to Miroslav Volf, who generously allowed me to sit in on a seminar where we discussed and met with Jürgen Moltmann, whose work influenced me greatly. I am particularly grateful to Ray Anderson, who took me under his wing when what I wanted to do didn't quite fit Fuller's program at the time. As a student, Ray's very method of theologizing was so captivating that all I wanted was to do the same. Ray later graciously encouraged me to work with Robert Banks when the new concentration in practical theology was developed. Rob's life work in home churches stirred me to consider community as the center of the Christian life and ministry (even in larger churches), and through his humility, candor, and attention to detail he prodded me to my best effort. I was deeply moved by Rob's extraordinary commitment to me, particularly through the painful time during the illness and after the passing of his first wife, Julie, just as my dissertation was being completed. Thank you, Rob. You will always be a model of service and magnanimity to me.

During the time that I have been working on this project, I have been privileged to serve in two different churches. The First Presbyterian Church of Hollywood was a wonderful place to learn the ropes of ministry. They were my first community. I am particularly grateful that God allowed me to serve during this formative time in my life with Lloyd John Ogilvie as my senior pastor. At a time when many were telling me to decide between academics and pastoring, Lloyd charged me to do both. I remain in your debt, Lloyd.

When I was called to become the pastor and head of staff for San Clemente Presbyterian, they eagerly embraced both my family and my vision of the church being a community of spiritual formation in Christ. And while I came with the baggage of needing considerable time off to complete my degree, they didn't begrudge a conflict of my attention. They graciously paid for my last three seminars, gave me a summer of study leave, and encouraged me with their prayers and well wishes. Bruce and Louise Brown and Al and Enid Sloan gave me places to write in their homes that were not only inspiring with ocean views, but conveniently close to my family.

As the dissertation went through a lengthy revision for publication as a book, I once again felt the support of this wonderful community of faith. My administrative assistant, Barbara Young, and pastoral executive staff team of Dee Hazen, Don Nieman, Jim Toole, and Shawn Reilly are so competent and supportive that I was allowed ample time for writing and revisions. Jim also read the manuscript in its entirety and offered helpful suggestions along the way. Thank you all for all you do for our church and for me.

My elders worked through ten weeks of lectures as I struggled to make the mystery of the Trinity relevant to intelligent and faithful lay leaders who are dedicated to seeing the church reflect the character of God. Their questions made my book stronger; their commitment to leading our church as a life-transforming community has brought the words of these pages to life and immense joy to my heart.

My sister, Carrie Nahmias, painstakingly transcribed my lectures, and Rob Asghar helped me edit them into a book format. Rob served as my "literary physical trainer," pushing me and stretching me to find a voice for integrating theology into church life. Rob's editorial skill, keen mind, probing questions, and deep belief in the message of this book was the single biggest factor for bringing what had been a mostly academic discussion to pastors and lay leaders.

Rodney Clapp, Rebecca Cooper, and Don Stephenson of Brazos Press have been strong and supportive editors, cheerleaders, and critics. I have grown as a writer from working with them and consider it a privilege to be part of the company of authors whom they represent. Don's encouragement of my writing has been a blessing to me indeed.

Throughout the years of development, one friend has stood with me the closest. When I was just beginning my Ph.D. program, Mark Roberts was finishing his dissertation in New Testament from Harvard. As the pastor of Irvine Presbyterian Church, Mark understands like few others the specific struggles that accompany trying to combine family life, writing, and pastoring. All along the way, Mark has been a loving goad and an understanding friend—never letting me get distracted for too long from the goal that was ahead of me. In our families, our ministries, and our shared love for learning and teaching the faith, Mark has been a "best friend" for me. I don't know how I can be so blessed.

Finally, the center of my life is a communion that is so sweet and tender, so fun and fulfilling that I ache because I have not the words to describe it. My two children, Brooks and Ali, have never known a time when Dad wasn't both a pastor and a writer. They love our church and inspire me to do all in my power to insure that it is a good community for them and the whole generation of their little friends who call me "Pastor Tod." My kids also offer me ample amounts of loving teasing when I am too focused on the computer screen and need to come out and play.

And lastly, to my dear, sweet Beth, the love of my life: you deserve so much more than any mention in these pages. You are my partner in building a community of faith that resembles the love of our Lord. We have been married nearly as long as I have worked on this book, and you have believed in me and protected our ministry and our life together. You deserve far more than my love and gratitude, my respect and constant goofy gaze. You deserve far more than having this book dedicated to you. But it is.

Through all of these, I have experienced what I learned in others' writings: that the *essence* of God is the love that is shared by the Persons of the Trinity, demonstrated in Jesus Christ and poured into our hearts by the Holy Spirit—and that love, when expressed by the communion of believers, transforms. I may not adequately explain the "transforming communion," but I have experienced it.

Introduction

A Latté, Some Friends, and the Trinity

I have always been jealous of the Inklings. I wish that I could have been part of that group of friends who met to talk about God, literature, and life that included J. R. R. Tolkien and C. S. Lewis. I can only imagine how stimulating it would have been to be part of that ongoing conversation. I love conversation. And maybe because of that jealousy, I am trying to reproduce a coffee shop conversation in this book. It is the kind of conversation that my colleagues and I have in the afternoons when we need to get out of the church office for a few minutes. We'll certainly talk about God and life, but we'll do so by focusing on theology and the church.

Let me then welcome you, the reader, to the conversation. Please consider sitting down with a cup of coffee, a pen to scribble in the margins, and maybe a partner or two to read along with. I intend this book for pastors and church leaders. It is also meant to be a frank and friendly argument with some writers whom I respect and enjoy.

In this conversation, I want to help move to the forefront of our thinking an ancient biblical imperative. It hasn't been rejected so much as ignored or forgotten. But it is critical nonetheless: *As God is, so the church should be. As God does, the church should do.* With the result being that *the more the church is like God, the more individual souls will become like Christ.*

The primary purpose of this book is not to stimulate theological argument, but to influence change at the level of congregational daily living. It is offered for the specific intention of assisting pastors and church leaders to create the kind of Christian communities in which God mystically transforms believers *together* into the likeness of Christ as the primary means for reaching a lost world. *Indeed, forming people into exceptional Christians—persons able to model Christian faith effectively to seekers—requires forming exceptional communities.*

This book offers a vision and some suggestions for "an exceptional Christian life." We will examine the challenges in creating a theology that makes a difference by making people different, and we will explore some practical communal applications. But first, let me invite some other participants to the table for this conversation.

First are some classic teachers and scholars of the faith, most significantly John Calvin. Calvin is a second-generation Reformer who built on the work of first-generation Reformers like Martin Luther by applying it to everyday life. Frankly, Calvin was not nearly as interesting a person as Luther. Luther was brash and bold, passionate and bombastic, and could tell an off-color joke. Calvin was hardly the life of the party. A former lawyer who secretly pined for a life of quiet study, Calvin had a great mind, a high sense of morals and ethics, and a desire to see Christians live holy lives. Calvin is often called the "theologian of the Holy Spirit," writing more about the practical dimensions of living the Christian life than about any other subject.[1] While we will also hear from Augustine, Luther, Karl Barth, and some contemporary theologians, if anybody is the moderator of this little roundtable, it is surely the Doctor from Geneva.

The second group is made up of contemporary writers of Christian spirituality. These soul instructors have taught us how to pray, to develop spiritual disciplines, and to seek the deeper things of the Spirit that transform our lives. For most evangelicals, Richard Foster, Dallas Willard, Henri Nouwen and others like them have restored to us what was common knowledge in generations past: the way that God intends to shape human souls. First as a disciple of Christ and second as a pastor, I have been changed for good by these teachers. They have shown me the way to a deeper Christian life that can handle the "dark nights of the soul," the crises of faith, and the struggle of prayer. They have enabled me to lead others to a richer life with Christ that is rooted like a giant oak amid the storms of life. But very often when I try to offer their wisdom to the "everyday" Christian sitting in the pew, it is, sadly, silently rejected.

Recent evangelical books on spirituality have argued for spiritual formation and discipleship to become more than an "elective" in church life but have yet to provide a comprehensive model for doing so.[2] The result is that their lessons have often been treated as kind of an "advanced class" for those who are more dedicated or more spiritually able than the soccer mom, CEO, recent retiree, or struggling young adult who is just trying to live the Christian life amid the pushes and pulls of our culture.

These "ordinary" people certainly wish they had time or inclination to spend an hour in prayer every day, to fast regularly, to journal pages of soul-searching dialogue, or to spend a weekend on a private retreat. But they just can't. Or won't. That may be good for monks, they say, but I have kids and a career, aging parents and a house to clean.

So they go to church, listen to the sermon, and try to live faithfully until the next infusion of spiritual assistance. With all due respect to the teachers of spiritual disciplines, they will stick with their usual Christian routine. For these "normal" Christians, there is some degree of disappointment with these teachers. A frustration that they are almost too embarrassed to admit: How can I be transformed? How can I become more like Christ when I am just not able to be so "spiritual"?

So, I want to point the conversation about the human soul in a more *churchly* direction. What are the spiritual practices of the *normal* congregation for shaping souls? What should be the spiritual disciplines that we practice as a church for ensuring that our members are transformed to be more like Jesus? In short, does the well-intended Presbyterian sitting in my church pew have to go off and "play Catholic or Quaker" on the weekend?

Although recent books for church leaders have drawn from the success and story of particular congregations,[3] these books put forth a programmatic agenda that while helpful is less theologically rooted and widely applicable. This book, too, has been shaped through the life of one congregation, the 1,200-member San Clemente Presbyterian Church in south Orange County, California. From time to time, I will draw on my church's experience to illustrate my points. Our vision statement declares our intention to be a

> *"Community for the community":* a multi-generational, life-transforming, unwaveringly Christ-centered Community of people who, together, worship the Triune God, proclaim and demonstrate the Good News of God, and provide every person in the greater San Clemente area a place to belong in the family of God, a place to grow in Jesus Christ, and a place to serve by the leading and the power of the Holy Spirit.

It will include some of the "church's story." But in a day in which there are ample discussions about "church things" (worship styles, organizational strategies, denominational structures, cell groups), church environments (seeker-friendly, user-friendly, purpose-driven, mega-churches), and church goals (numerical growth, spiritual growth, theological fidelity, mission and evangelism), there has been a gross misunderstanding of what the church *is.* And that is what I want to talk about over this cup (or several cups) of coffee.

The third group with whom I want to dialogue is the church strategists. Dynamic pastors and insightful experts, they have looked at the way that the church has become irrelevant to so many people—so boring, so "foreign"—and they have tried to reshape the church along more intentionally evangelistic lines. They have made the church more "user-friendly," "seeker-sensitive," "purpose-driven." And I applaud them. I am not among those who criticize the mega-churches for being too "polished" or too focused on the unsaved. As a pastor, I have learned a great deal about the way that the church often turns away the very people we say we are trying to attract. I have gratefully infused my discussions with church leaders with the concepts these people teach, and we have reached more people for Christ. Indeed, the San Clemente congregation has doubled in size and budget in the past six years.

But, I also want to point the discussion in a more *theological* direction concerned with the ultimate purpose for saved individuals. This is not to say that I question the theology of these colleagues. Indeed, we share many of the same core beliefs. I just want to focus our attention on *ecclesiology, the theology of the church*.

With membership dwindling in most mainline denominations and individual churches, an optimist might assert that mega-churches are drawing huge crowds, that the Christian events have filled stadiums, and that sales of Christian music and merchandise have reached all-time highs. But there is, of course, a crucial difference between a *crowd* and a *community*. That is where a number of would-be models for twenty-first-century Christianity get it wrong, and that is one of the key themes of this book. For many churches, the main goal is to build a big crowd, and community is tacked onto the bargain (usually in the form of a small group), the way that medical benefits and vacation days are tacked onto a job offer. But while *crowds* come and go, true and enduring Christian *community* is a foretaste of heaven, the essence of the discipleship, the enduring witness to an unbelieving world, and an absolute necessity for human transformation.

Even more subtly, but importantly, there is an enduring difference between a *collective* of individual Christians and a *community*. Many pastors and lay leaders talk the right talk—about needing to be relational rather than programmatic—but they then get hopelessly lost in creating relational programs so that their collective of individual Christians will have a sense of connection to each other. However, the fundamental reality of the church as an enduring, covenantal, irreducible, and Trinity-reflecting entity *in and of itself* is overlooked entirely. As Emil Brunner wrote a half century ago in *The Misunderstanding of the Church,* "togetherness of Christians is . . . not secondary or contingent: it is integral to their life just as is their abiding in Christ."[4]

Certainly, some recent books on small groups and Christian community[5] have rightly emphasized the loneliness and lack of intimacy among Christians. But they have neglected the transformative power of Christian community. In many ways, my critique is similar to sociologist Robert Wuthnow's critique of the small-group movement. Wuthnow warned that in the midst of all the affirmation for the millions of people involved in small groups, the movement itself was far too oriented toward individual needs. Small groups became simply a part of an individual's personal "do-it-yourself" religion that reinforced "individualized faith." The most common reason why people say they join and stay with small groups is for what they receive for their own highly personalized needs and goals; small groups encourage a "private and inward focused" spirituality that also "permits traditional communities to be abandoned."[6]

But perhaps an even more important question to ask is whether our church strategies are a genuine reflection of who *God* is. You see, *while I believe that the church strategists have accurately described the starting place for a church that intentionally embodies the mission of God, they have lost sight of the finish line.* For all the genuine good that we have learned from marketing and management, isn't there something in the very nature or spiritual makeup of the church that makes it a unique group of people? Isn't there a purpose for the church that is beyond *my* finding *my* purpose for living? Isn't the church first and foremost about God and not us—and dare I say—*not* the seeker? And if so, so what?

For most Christians, both new guests and church leaders, the local church is usually regarded as a benign reality. We honor the church and may even use the traditional language in declaring it a "means of grace." But most often we think of the church as a "strategy" or a "system" for local evangelistic efforts and social change, or as a dispenser of resources to help the individual on his or her Christian journey. Churches are offered like different shops are offered at a mall. Indeed, the largest churches offer themselves *as* a kind of spiritual mall entire, bidding the seeker: *Come here and choose from our wide array of Christian classes, teachings, and activities that you need to live out your individual Christian life*. In this model, the church is a repository of spiritual goods that assist the individual Christian. It is a vendor of religious services. It is the Home Depot for the spiritual do-it-yourselfer who wants to build a Christian home. But that is not the church of the first century. *The church of the first century is "a people."* And the transformed and transforming quality of "the people" serving as the flesh-and-blood witness to a life-transforming God is the point. As 1 Peter 2:9–10 (NLT) says:

> You are a chosen people. You are a kingdom of priests, God's holy nation, his very own possession. This is so you can show others the goodness of God, for he called you out of the darkness into his wonderful light.
>
> "Once you were not a people;
> now you are the people of God.

Once you received none of God's mercy;
now you have received mercy."

This is what I want to remind us of in this book: The church is God's incarnation today. The church is Jesus' body on earth. The church is the temple of the Spirit. The church is not a helpful thing for my individual spiritual journey. The church *is* the journey. The church is not a collection of "soul-winners" all seeking to tell unbelievers "the Way" to God. The church *is* the Way. To be part of the church is to be part of God—to be part of God's Communion and to be part of God's ministry. To belong to the people of God is to enjoy relationship with God and live out the purposes of God. The church is God's present-day word and witness to an unbelieving world.[7] And, most importantly, the church is the only true means to be transformed to into the likeness of God.

The starting point of felt needs, cultural factors, and contemporary relevance cannot and should not be ignored, but neither should the final vision for which we are elected and saved, and toward which we must journey. The church is Christ's body, the dwelling place or temple of God, and a reflection of God on earth.

There is a fourth group I'd like to invite into this discussion. While I doubt many will read a book like this, their questions and criticisms spawned it in the first place. It is the vast number of people who consider themselves seekers. More than at almost any time in history, ours is a nation of spiritual seekers. Millions are hungering for meaning and hungering to be changed—to discover fully who they were meant to be and to find their place within the human community. Yet this opportunity is also a problem. The Christian church is not a destination for many of these seekers, because they suspect—and the evidence supports their view—that Christians are not changed people. We claim that Christ is the only way to an exceptional life, yet studies indicate that we, on the whole, live very similarly to those who do not profess a faith in Christ. We are called the "body of Christ," and yet we don't seem very much like Christ.

Here, then, is the imperative and the opportunity. As theologian G. C. Berkouwer declared, one of the "aims of the church" is the sanctification of the individual, so that the children of God will be "seen as lights in the world"[8] (cf. Phil. 2:15; Zech. 8:23; Matt. 5:14–16). To seekers as well as to its own flock, the church must now announce, "If you desire a transformed life, you must be transformed within the church. If you desire to be changed people, you must change the church. If you would find your life, you must lose it within a redeemed and redemptive community that together lives the manner of abundant and exceptional life that God intended for us."

Throughout this writing, I have been inspired by a fifteenth-century icon, *The Holy Trinity,* painted by Andrei Rublev.[9] In it, the Father, Son, and Holy Spirit sit together at a table, demonstrating the Divine Communion that is the foundation of the world. The center of focus is a chalice of wine representing Christ's blood. It sits in the center as a single shared cup, bidding us to come, partake, and—in doing so—share in the fellowship and redemptive activity of God. The true center of the Divine Communion thus is a shared sacrificial love that manifests in the world. When it is poured out, it reveals the true character of the communion for which our souls are restless, to which we are invited, and in which life is found.

PART 1

In Search of Exceptional Lives

1

It Takes a Church to Raise a Christian

What Are You Really Looking For?

> Now, the Lord is the spirit, and where the Spirit of the Lord is, there is freedom. And all of us, with unveiled faces, seeing the glory of the Lord as though reflected in a mirror, are being transformed into the same image from one degree of glory to another; for this comes from the Lord, the Spirit.
>
> 2 Corinthians 3:17–18

The musical group U2 sings a popular song with haunting lyrics. It is almost an anthem of our age. In a first-person, passionate declaration of his unsettled soul, lead singer Bono weaves a tale of climbing mountains, running through fields, scaling walls, running, breaking bonds, and carrying chains, only to end with this sorrowful declaration: *"But I still haven't found what I'm looking for."*

So let me ask you: What are you looking for? What do you want at the deepest core of your being? I know what I want. And I'll bet it's what you want, too.

What we really want is to be accepted just as we are and to become all we are meant to be. We want to belong to a community that welcomes us in all our painful brokenness and helps us to be healed and transformed into more than we ever imagined. We all want to be loved and transformed by love.

In fact, while the Bible makes a number of eyebrow-raising claims, the most provocative one is that Christians are a people who will be changed dramatically—not only on the other side of the grave, but in significant measure here and now. My primary thesis is that the change we most yearn for is available to us only through the Triune God who transforms his people within the divine community, the church—The People of the Table. I believe and want to convince you that "it takes a church to raise a Christian."

Admittedly, that's a play on words on an African proverb that also inspired a former first lady, Hillary Rodham Clinton. The proverb says, "It takes a village to raise a child." In a similar way that the proverb reveals the necessity of a community to raise healthy children in an often hostile world, the process of spiritual growth and transformation is an even more intensely communal activity. Indeed, it is the primary activity of a God who is Communion in his very being, who by his saving deeds has offered eternal life to all people within the Divine Communion of his people.

But, as we will see, there is a considerable chasm separating us from who we are—I mean "we" as a corporate people, we as the indivisible body of Christ—and who we are to become. While we may be saved from hell and assured that we'll never be separated from God, we aren't living the manner of life we were built for, we aren't making the difference that we could make together, and we're not drawing people to the form of life-giving fellowship that they and we crave.

This has always flummoxed Christian leaders, whether illustrated by Paul admonishing the Corinthian church, John Calvin fretting as he walked the streets of Geneva, or ministers in our own day lamenting our lapse in values. But the problem is especially tough today. That's because real godly change—real sanctification—requires a people to live together in covenantal relationships, and we're less inclined to that than any generation in human history.

More than any before us, an American today believes "I must write the script of my own life." The thought that such a script must be subordinated to the grand narrative of the Bible is a foreign one. Still more alarming is the idea that this surrender of our personal story to God's story must be mediated by a community of fallen people we frankly don't want getting in our way and meddling with our own hopes and dreams.

And in a culture that tells us to march on with ever greater self-reliance and self-expression, the Bible tells us that the story of our life is not our own, and our journey is not our own. God the Father, Son, and Holy Spirit and his people come along with us (or, to put it a little more accurately, we go along with them). And along that journey, a God who is inherently community changes our human community into his image.

This can't be explained easily or quickly. There are so many nuances that affect our church life that I must ask you to bear with me for the next two hundred pages. We will study in some depth three theological concepts:

1. God as Trinity
2. The church as community
3. The goal of humanity as transformation

We will see that full human transformation requires understanding, believing, and living out the consequences of all three concepts. I will begin by introducing each one briefly.

Grasping the Trinity

To be a Christian, one must believe in the Trinity. So, when asked, we affirm it absolutely, even singing with all our hearts the old hymn and its mellifluous words: "Holy, holy, holy, blessed Trinity." But most of us have no idea what it means.

One of my goals is to make the concept of the Trinity exciting—or at least a bit more accessible and useful. Some points will resonate immediately, while others will not. But let us persist: the theology of the Trinity is extremely important because it describes the God whom we love and serve! Happily, the theology addressed is actually a good deal simpler than it may appear at first glance. Essentially, what we will see is that because God is a Trinity, the essence of God is loving relationship, best understood as communion. Therefore, the essence of humanity, as God's creation, is also relationship.

This can be very difficult for us modern Westerners to grasp. In cultures where identity is tied to family relationships, trinitarian relationship and identity is more easily understood and accepted. But we have been so steeped in individualism that we forget that even the Lone Ranger had Tonto. We naturally believe that the very essence of humanity is the individual will. Truly understanding who God is is absolutely necessary for understanding who we are and who we are meant to become.

The Church as Community

Second, I will tap into our current cultural hunger for community and demonstrate how Christian community is the only truly life-transforming environment. But first, let's define what I mean by *community.* Our culture is currently undergoing a period of nostalgia for the day in which neighbors and families were stable, knew each other well, and cared for one another through the ups and downs of life. Many social commentators are trying to restore the ideal of civic community to American public life, and I deeply understand and applaud their efforts. But Christian community is not just about neighborliness (though certainly the gospel demands that we "love our neighbors"), nor is it just about proximity (though without proximity community is impossible). It's not just being friends or living in the same housing development. It's about sharing *more* than a cup of sugar and the lawn mower: sharing core values and a vision for living.

What this means is that the church in its essence is not an organization, even a helpful, divinely mandated one. Contrary to what many of us have been taught, the church is not just a means of grace; and the church is not just here to help you in your individual journey of faith.

I remember sitting in evangelistic meetings as a young Christian hearing several well-meaning preachers (later, I myself was one such, I must admit) saying, "All you have to do to be saved is to accept Jesus into your heart. There is no church to join. There's nothing to do. You can have a relationship with Jesus right here tonight all by yourself." Usually the preacher would suggest that a good Bible teaching church would be helpful to the new believer (as vitamins help a diet), but what was most important was a "personal relationship by asking Jesus into your heart."

Over time I have come to realize that Paul would never have preached that message. Instead, all of the early church preached, "Believe and be baptized." Have faith in Christ and join with the people of Christ. Know the God who is community and become part of it yourself.

Further, Christian community is not just a shared experience. It's not people who sit together in pews or a movie theater or a football stadium (even if they are the audience for a Christian event!). It's not polite conversation at a potluck or a great weekend together at a Christian camp. Christian community is an ontologically irreducible organism. It is a living reality that is imbued with the Spirit of God. And most dramatically, it is the very life of the Triune God drawing people into a covenantal relationship with God and one another. It is God's own being on earth lived in and through believers for the single end result of seeing each person become like Jesus Christ. Thus, the community together is a witness for Christ.

Why Are We Still Here?

Third, the purpose of God for humanity is the whole-life transformation of every person into the likeness of the Triune God through the divine community. When I was a teenaged new Christian, I once asked my youth leader why God kept Christians on earth after they were saved. I remember thinking that if the reason why Jesus went to the cross was to save us from hell and make it possible for us to live with God for eternity in heaven, then why didn't we all just convert and then commit suicide? I wasn't really interested in suicide, but I was interested in figuring out "Why am I still here?"

The usual answer given was, "As a believer, you are to stay on earth and lead other people to Jesus also." This made some sense, except that I wasn't a particularly good evangelist, and I knew a lot of Christians were even worse than I was. That answer led me to ask sarcastically if there should be an evangelism aptitude test given to every Christian. All the ones who are good at leading people to Jesus would stay on earth, and everyone else would immediately go to heaven. Doesn't that make sense? If the purpose for humanity is going to heaven, then maybe Billy Graham and some other evangelists should stay here—but the rest of us aren't needed.

The problem, of course, is in the assumption. Because the purpose of humanity is not to escape hell, and the reason Jesus came to earth was not simply to save us for eternity after we die. Jesus didn't go to the cross as fire insurance. The purpose of God's plan from the very beginning of time was not that you'd make it to heaven; it was that you'd be like Christ. God's divine intention for humanity is transforming us into the likeness of Christ, who was the Triune God in human flesh. In the words of Romans 8:29: "For those whom he foreknew he also predestined to be conformed to the image of his Son . . ."

I heard of a church that has a sign over the nursery based on 1 Corinthians 15:51: "They will not all sleep, but they will all be changed." While humorous, given the context of a nursery, this verse is the truth of the gospel. Even more certain than death is the transformation of every Christian into the likeness of Christ. We may not all die (that is, if Christ returns beforehand), but if we are in Christ, we will all be changed. In 2 Corinthians 3:17 Paul writes that the purpose of the Holy Spirit in the world is our transformation into the likeness of Christ.

Peter Drucker notes that the bottom line of a for-profit corporation is, not surprisingly, a healthy profit. But what about a nonprofit organization? What about a school, a hospital, a charitable foundation, or a church? If the "bottom line" is not a healthy profit, then what is it? Says Drucker, the bottom line of a nonprofit organization is to fulfill its mission to bring about changed human lives.[1] But I want to quickly add that, in the case of a church, the bottom line is changed human lives according to the image of Jesus. The whole purpose of church work and life is that people's lives will be transformed to reflect and reveal Jesus Christ. Throughout this book I'll discuss what I mean by that, but it is inspired by a very personal and deeply communal mental picture.

My family moved to San Clemente when my daughter, Ali, was only three months old. Today she is bright, precocious, and full of spunk. An elementary-school child who loves to laugh, learn, and tease her daddy. As a very proud father, I must admit sheepishly that I sometimes envision her someday becoming our church's senior pastor. Mostly, I like to think about the effect of her living her life completely within our church community and to imagine the kind of person she could become through the prayers, friendship, nurture, and admonition of this body.

Like all parents, I pray that my daughter will have a long, happy life. I trust that I will someday precede her into eternity, and I dream of the day when the word will come to me that my daughter has also arrived at the pearly gates. I will rush to meet her, and as I approach I will see two resplendent figures standing together. I will squint to recognize her, because she will have been so transformed into the image of Jesus by the love and nurture of our community that I will be unable to tell them apart. Finally, I dream that I have to ask, "Please tell me, which one of you is my daughter, and which one of you is my Lord?"

That is sanctification, the transformation of a person into the likeness of Jesus Christ, through the work and life of a Christian community. My dream is that if my daughter lived her whole life as a member of San Clemente Presbyterian Church, from three months to the day she goes to glory, that her transition to glory would be so easy, so minimal, because the life and love of our community will have transformed her into the image of Christ to a significant degree before she sees him face-to-face.

But this vision is not just for my daughter. Or just for Christians. It is what God intends for every person. I believe, in the words from my denomination's constitution, that "the Church of Jesus Christ is the provisional demonstration of what God intends for all humanity."[2] In other words, God's intention is that the church is meant to demonstrate what God intends for everyone until the day comes when everyone will live as God intended.

So as we learn how to be a life-transforming community, we do so for both those who share the faith and—perhaps more importantly—those who are still seeking. My hope is that this book will help the church fulfill its calling so that that every one of us—"you, for your children, and for all who are far away, everyone whom the Lord our God calls to him" (Acts 2:39)—will experience the life-transforming love of Jesus Christ.

2

Come for Supper!

> If Christianity is what it claims to be, then it should be producing a type and order of life which is quite exceptional. If therefore, we are to meet the challenge of the modern world we must be living the Christian life; and the question arises how we are to do so.[1]
>
> Martyn Lloyd-Jones

Today, like most days, people will gather around tables. Coffee tables, drawing tables, breakfast and dinner tables, boardroom tables, picnic tables, and school tables. Families will discuss problems, joys and the details of the day. Deals will be made and divorce settlements finalized. Papers will be signed and friendships will be renewed. Milk will be spilt and puzzles will be built, homework will be done and bills will be left unpaid. The table, maybe more than any other item, is universal, necessary, and ordinary. It is around tables that life is lived, and it is at tables that, perhaps unexpectedly, God can be found.

There seems to be a lot of interest in finding God or something like God these days. I read the statistics. I watch television shows. I listen to popular music. There is no mistaking the fact that people are searching for the sacred. Every day, I see a seeking world of people, who in the words of an old country-western song, are "looking for love in all the wrong places." Unfortunately, most are not looking in Christian churches. At least, not often or for long. The world is seeking a connection with the divine, and the church is missing a grand opportunity.

Why is this? Here's the brutal fact: we are not that different from them, and so what we offer them is not that different from what they can find in a host of other places in our culture.

Because you are reading this book, chances are good that you're a pastor, church leader, missionary, Sunday school teacher or some other manner of faithful Christian who has experienced the same frustration. After counseling a couple whose marriage doesn't seem to get better, after teaching a lesson on holiness, after begging for people to offer more of themselves to the church or to reach out to neighbors with the love of Christ, you find yourself sitting over coffee, brooding, "How come we're not better than this?" Legend holds that John Calvin used to walk the streets of Geneva after the Reformation had taken place, after everybody had been converted to the Protestant faith, muttering, "Why can't they be good?"

It is tempting to see these questions as nothing more than theological self-indulgence, churchly navel-gazing. We are tempted to "look on the bright side," to quiet that disappointed inner voice. But we can't. Not if we are going to be true to who we are. We may never have heard the quote before, but somewhere in our guts we know that the church—that messy bunch of quasi-hypocritical, well-intentioned, and mostly off-key do-gooders—in the words of Dietrich Bonhoeffer, *is* Christ in the world today.[2] There is no Jesus here but us, and we are being challenged by a world seeking for Jesus.

The Challenge and the Gap

> (People) are hungry, spiritually malnourished. People want to grow spiritually above all else.[3]

On November 28, 1994, *Newsweek* magazine ran as its cover story "The Search for the Sacred: America's Quest for Spiritual Meaning."[4] Almost thirty years after *Time* magazine asked "Is God Dead?" *Newsweek*'s religion editor, Kenneth L. Woodward, wrote, "What Americans seem to be searching for is some sense of harmony with a cosmic order and communion with its source—the experience other societies have celebrated as the presence of the sacred."[5] Indeed, as one sociologist notes, spiritual seeking is now an enduring part of the American psyche. "People now take pride in the fact that they are spiritually seeking."[6]

What is vexing is that studies have shown that amid all the excitement of our culture's growing openness to spiritual things, there is a sobering and disturbing sense that Christianity appears increasingly irrelevant to the myriad of spiritual seekers.[7] Notwithstanding the temporary flocking to American churches after September 11, 2001, Christianity has shown no demonstrable growth in numbers or influence within the culture.[8] Even worse, while Americans are seeking God, they are by and large not seeking God in Christian churches.[9] As Leonard Sweet declares, "there is a huge spiritual hunger (in postmodern culture) and at the same time a rejection of Christianity as the kind of spirituality that can slake spiritual hunger." Current popular spiritualities pose not only an opportunity, but also perhaps one of the greatest challenges to Christianity today.[10]

But why is this so?

A full half-century ago, Martyn Lloyd-Jones wrote that the key strategy for Christianity to make a difference in the world is to produce exceptional lives: lives that would be self-commending . . . "and the question arises how we are to do so." In short, we meet the challenge of a world of seekers by our lives. We are to be a living representation of what they seek.

Yet, in a world faced with spiritual seekers, it seems unfortunately like Christianity is not as commendable as we might hope.[11] Mainline denominations are in decline,[12] and evangelical churches, growing in numbers, have been shocked to find that their members demonstrate little difference in lifestyle, beliefs, and commitments from those of non-Christians. Those who profess Christian faith have almost exactly the same lifestyle patterns as unbelievers. Our divorce rates, our amount of extramarital sex, of suicide, of alcohol abuse, of drug abuse, of depression is virtually the same as those of non-Christians. And as our newspapers are filled with the scandals of the church, with cynicism about religion at an all-time high, where clergy are equivalent in esteem and respect to car salesmen and lawyers, the question arises: "What difference are we making in the world?"

As two observers have noted, "While religion is highly popular in America, it is to a large extent superficial; it does not change people's lives to the degree one would expect from their level of professed faith."[13] Dallas Willard points out:

> We have counted on preaching and teaching to form faith in the hearer, and on faith to form the inner life and ordered behavior of the Christian. But for whatever reason, this strategy has not turned out well. The result is that we have multitudes of professing Christians that well may be ready to die, but obviously are not ready to live, and can hardly get along with themselves, much less others.[14]

But how did this come to be so? Writing in 1973, Richard Lovelace identified a "sanctification gap" within Protestant theology, teaching, and preaching. According to Lovelace, for most of Christian history before the Enlightenment, the study and teaching of theology had a distinctly, if not always intentionally, practical and spiritual aim. Pastors learned theology so that they could help their flocks grow spiritually. The goal of the pastoral work was to teach spiritual wisdom and foster spiritual maturity.[15]

Historically, the way the pastor formed spiritual maturity in believers was to form, care for, and mature a distinctly Christian community.[16] The doctrine of sanctification, that is, the spiritual growth of the believer, was from the very beginning of the New Testament understood to be a natural result of a maturing Christian community. Indeed, in his discussion of New Testament ethics, Richard Hays demonstrates that the community, not the individual, is the "primary addressee of God's imperatives," in order to form a Christian community as an "alternative order" witnessing to the life-changing presence of God.[17] This is good news to us, because recent studies have revealed that while Christian belief alone doesn't lead to demonstrably different lifestyle choices than those made by non-Christians, regular churchgoers do show a marked increase in charitable giving and involvement in environmental causes, civic duties, volunteerism, and other socially desirable activities, as well as significantly lower levels of drug and alcohol abuse, promiscuity, and other social ills.[18]

Unfortunately, the life-transforming effect of biblical sanctification nurtured in Christian community has been overlooked by both theologians and pastors. Because of a myriad of issues from theology to politics, as theology moved through the Enlightenment and into the twentieth century, the doctrine of sanctification was greatly ignored in theological education and Christian preaching and teaching.[19] More and more scholars focused upon theology as a distinct field of academic inquiry and increasingly ignored its practical and communal character.

Increasingly, the very framing of theological issues (doctrinal defense), the method of framing theological problem (through polemical systematic theology), and the desired outcomes (reinforcing of or creating restatements of doctrinal formulation) led in exactly the opposite direction of our earliest theology. Instead of becoming a practical, formational, and communal theological expression, theology became more and more divorced from ministry and less applicable to the building of a distinctively Christian community.[20]

Even within evangelicalism, with the phenomenon of the megachurch, there is widespread agreement about the great degree of unexceptional Christian living and deficiency of spiritual depth. As former Regent University professor of spiritual theology, James Houston comments,

> In spite of the renewal movements, there is a dearth today of spiritual leadership in the evangelical world. . . . Evangelical Protestants are largely secularized by their politics, their obsessions with growth, and their interests in administration and parachurch activities. The loss of the practice of prayer, the ignorance of the rich traditions of spirituality, and the need to develop a cultural framework for the practice of devotion are challenges worthy of the most serious consideration.[21]

We have ignored the ancient wisdom of sanctification, spirituality, and building community and have focused instead on building crowds of the nominally converted.[22] Alister McGrath observes that "evangelicalism is seen to lack a spirituality to give its theology staying power in the modern period."[23] We have forgotten how to form exceptional lives.

Now, to be clear, I am not opposed to making our churches more effective or even more attractive to outsiders. As noted earlier, I'm not in any way critical of churches that are actively reaching out to the unchurched. But as wisdom has been replaced with technique, there has been less demonstrable lasting spiritual growth in Christians and little measurable cultural impact.[24] The seekers of the world report that the church addresses their substantial spiritual needs with superficial theology, superficial programs, and superficial believers. They come hungering for a spiritual feast, and we offer them salad bars.

Salad-Bar Spirituality

When I was in high school, I worked at a restaurant that boasted of having the best salad bar in town. While salad bars haven't quite the same popularity today, they were huge for most of the 1980s and early 1990s. What was not to like? Nutritious food, wide variety, bite-sized, convenient, take exactly what you want, when you want it. Everyone in the family could get whatever he or she wanted. Indeed, a famous chain of restaurants developed an advertisement that seemed to capture the popularity of the salad bar perfectly: Three well-dressed professionals, all walking at a brisk pace heading off to lunch, saying over and over again, "I don't have a lot of time; I don't want to spend a lot of money."

It seemed that the salad bar was perfect for us. And in many ways, this is a perfect metaphor for spiritual seekers who approach faith in the same way:

"I don't have a lot of time; I don't want it to cost me much."

Of course, the desire to reach these people means that we pastors mostly try to cater to these folks. We offer lots of choices of programs with low commitment, have tapes available so that busy people can get "fed" on the go, communicate that Bible studies and small groups, service and giving, are "extras" and that you can have a "pay-as-you-go" mentality. We recognize that people are going to feed themselves spiritually from lots of different churches—maybe a Bible study that fits their schedule at the Baptist church, worship that they like at the Presbyterian church, and a support group at Calvary Chapel. Thus, Salad-Bar Christianity is born.

This isn't a condemnation. All things considered, I think that is a pretty good strategy for exposing people to the gospel and introducing them to Jesus and the Christian life. If we are going to help people take the first steps of faith, we should cater to them a bit, make the spiritual life as accessible and convenient as possible.

But does salad-bar Christianity create truly healthy, growing Christians? And while the world claims to want quick and inexpensive spiritual offerings, do they actually line up to be fed this type of spiritual meal? In short, is this what spiritual seekers are really seeking?

The restaurant I worked at went out of business, and the last I heard, the entire chain went bankrupt. This may seem surprising to us. We have neither more time nor money that we did twenty-five years ago. But I believe that reasons for the unexpected demise of the salad bar can be traced to some very human conditions . . . and that the end of restaurants like the one I worked at has something to say to us about what we expect from the spiritual life.

In his book *Exit Interviews,* William Hendricks revealed the results of interviews with people who have left the Christian church. Their reasons for leaving were varied, but two common themes were found:

1. When people leave the church, they are not trying to leave God.
2. When people leave the church, they are usually deeply disappointed in the church because *people in the church weren't religious enough and they couldn't find a sense of true community.*[25]

We might guess that they left because the preachers talked about tithing or because the sermons demanded too much, in the way that the crowds around Jesus diminished because of the demands of the discipleship. But no. One of the most significant complaints is that Christian churches don't deliver what they promise. There's no divine mystery unveiled, no genuine community demonstrated, they complained. Showing up at a church makes the same difference as showing up at any other social gathering. The church is the Kiwanis Club with better music.

Yes, they came in muttering the salad-bar mantra of low investment, but what they wanted was a community of people demonstrably different from the culture around them. They came looking for camaraderie, community, and commitment—and left disappointed. They came secretly hoping to find something more than a group that would cater to their whims. And they didn't even know it.

What's missing in a spiritual diet of build-your-own-meals from the salad bar? What's wrong with a build-your-own-faith of different morsels here or there? Perhaps I can best describe it by finishing my busboy story.

The restaurant had two very loyal customers who were twins; a brother and a sister, who both had flaming red hair. We called them "The Reds." They were warmhearted and friendly regulars. They ate every lunch and every dinner at the restaurant, always ordering the same thing: large salad bar, iced tea, dessert.

One day, we put up a sign that said that the restaurant would be closed for Thanksgiving dinner so that the employees could spend the day with their families. The Reds protested: "Where will we spend Thanksgiving dinner?" You see, while they had plenty of opportunities to eat, they didn't know how to have a real meal. They didn't have relationships for a genuine family dinner. They had no place else to go; they truly were planning on spending Thanksgiving at the restaurant. All the relationships they had formed were the superficiality of people who had waited on them. They were customers to us. But, they protested, we were their friends. They had a deep hunger for more than a cheap salad bar where they could build whatever meal they chose. What they really wanted was someone who knew them well enough to invite them to supper.

Meals are more than food, and we are mostly fed by the company we with whom we eat. A steady diet of salad-bar Christianity will never feed the soul deeply because it is not a true dinner table. There is nothing to share, nothing to be part of, nothing to invest in, nothing to clean up or to contribute. People may say that they want little investment in spiritual things, but they are hungering for far more.

As much as I am drawn to a salad-bar approach to church, we need to recognize that something precious and crucial to the church is lost if all we think about is how to "get fed" as quickly, easily, and inexpensively as possible. That something is a genuine, life-transforming,

God-reflecting, Spirit-embodying Christian community. The kind of place that will love us as we are and help us become all that we were meant to be.

As the church has embraced a salad-bar approach to Christianity, it has lost the ability to truly nourish the Christian soul and demonstrate a different quality of life. And we are quickly becoming irrelevant to a whole host of people hungering for something of the divine.[26]

The Invitation to a Divine Dinner Table

As I think about the spiritual seekers out there frustrated at salad-bar Christianity, it is a powerful idea that the central image of the Christian life is a dinner table. What Jesus gave us when he left us was a meal. Don't ever forget that the "high tea" that most of us do once a month or so with a little tiny piece of bread and a little tiny cup is supposed to be a foretaste of the heavenly feast of the Lamb that we will celebrate for eternity. It is the most ordinary and extraordinary experience all at once. In the early church the Lord's Supper was celebrated every time they took bread, every time they took wine.[27] They believed that every time Christians share the cup and loaf with other people, we offer a remembrance of the Lord and are nourished by his Spirit, demonstrating in every part of our lives our connection to God and one another.

What we do when we are gathered on Sunday mornings is meant to be just a small foretaste of what Jesus intends for us all to be. And, as we shall see, our experience of the Lord's Supper—our living out the Lord's Supper—is to be the most central demonstration of what we offer to the world: life-transforming communion.

Second Corinthians 3:17–18 says:

> Now, the Lord is the spirit, and where the spirit of the Lord is, there is freedom. And all of us, with unveiled faces, seeing the glory of the Lord as though reflected in a mirror, are being transformed into the same image from one degree of glory to another, for this comes from the Lord, the Spirit.

This passage teaches us that the intent of the Spirit is to transform us through the face-to-face encounter with the glory or personal presence of the Lord. In his commentary on this passage John Calvin asks, "So where is the glory of the Lord reflected?" The answer? At the Communion table.[28]

For most of us, this is a most unexpected answer. So to explore it, we'll need to fully understand the spectacular intention of the Triune God.

PART 2

History and Theology: Forming Exceptional Lives

3

God's Spectacular Intention

Why were we created? What is our purpose? The Bible says that *it is to be the image of God, a living reflection of the God who is love.* But what does that mean? Let me begin by painting you a scenario that probably takes place every night in many suburban households in our country. Maybe even yours.

A husband comes home at 8 P.M., waves to the guard of his gated community, drives down the deserted street, and pulls up in front of his house. There is no one on the street at this time of night, but no matter; beyond their first names, he really doesn't know his neighbors anyway.

He pushes the garage-door opener and parks his car, closing the door behind him. He notices that his wife's car is gone, still at work. He yells to the kids, who don't hear him, because his son is lying on his bed listening to his Walkman while he plays a Sega game, and his daughter is busy chatting on the Internet with a made-up name and personality. The girl has been doing it since she got home from school, and if you asked her, she would tell you her "friends" in the chat room are by far her closest, even though she has never seen them and they don't know her name. They don't care what she looks like, or anything.

He checks on his mother, who lives with them. She is watching a home shopping network and comments that the pretty anchorwoman seems to be losing weight. She says that the next time she buys something, she'll ask about the anchorwoman's health, because the hosts all seem like such nice people.

He goes into the kitchen and checks the answering machine, where there is a message from his wife telling everybody to fend for themselves tonight, as she has a big client dinner. He grabs a drink and a leftover sandwich, and plops down in the den at his computer, where he sends an e-mail to his cyber-girlfriend. He has never touched her; indeed, they have never met, but they write back and forth each day, and it is the most meaningful conversation that he has in his life.

Rare? Maybe. Becoming more common? Certainly. At least if a number of current social commentators are correct. And it is hard to fathom a more contradictory vision of what human life is supposed to be.

When Mother Teresa first visited the United States, decades ago, she was asked by a well-meaning reporter if she was enjoying being in the United States, where the poverty was not as glaring as in her native Calcutta. It seemed a most benign question. Mother Teresa's ministry in Calcutta was to pick up, tend to, and care for the poorest of the poor, the dying and discarded in the streets of Calcutta.

But Mother Teresa responded that in the United States she had not seen the same poverty of body, but she had seen and despaired over the poverty of soul. She said that in the United States she had seen such terrible loneliness. Thirty years ago that loneliness was relegated mostly to convalescent homes and college dorms. Now it is the epidemic that is right behind the cell phones, full day planners, and manicured lawns of the middle and upper classes: the abject loneliness of people who live in cities teeming with people or, even worse, in homes where people are close but increasingly disconnected.

Where has all this disconnection and loneliness come from? From us. It is the logical extension of a most pervasive and unquestioned worldview that is so much a part of who we are that our trying to talk about it is like a fish trying to discuss water. A worldview that puts all the emphasis on the solitary person, a worldview that says that since we are created as individuals we must live as independently as possible in order to be fully human.

In his book *Habits of the Heart,* University of California sociologist Robert Bellah studied the primary commitments and core values of the American people, that is, the most cherished and dominant features of our worldview.[1] Bellah's research declared that the two primary commitments of Americans are forms of *individualism*. He called these two dominant worldviews:

- *Utilitarian Individualism*: If it works for me, then it is good; and
- *Expressive Individualism*: If it fulfills or satisfies me, then it is good.

It is as American as apple pie to be individuals, to go it alone, to stand on one's own two feet, to live by one's own existence. This is what freedom is all about, isn't it? According to Barry Shain's *The Myth of American Individualism,* the individualism we have today lies in the complete opposite direction of the intentions of our founders. Liberty for the early Americans did not mean complete freedom to be left alone, but instead the freedom to order one's life by the ethical demands of the Scriptures, confirmed by reason, within a community. The earliest Americans believed that true human freedom is possible only if it is lived out in a moral, tightly knit community. It is freedom with and for community.[2]

Our commitment to individualism has led to the breakdown of community and the disconnection of families, neighbors, and townspeople. In his book *Bowling Alone,* Robert Putnam charts the cultural breakdown of social clubs and organizations. While more people are bowling than ever before, fewer are bowling in leagues. While more people talk of the need for better education, fewer are involved in organizations like the PTA. While more people are interested in matters of religion, fewer are inclined to join churches.[3] Mars Hill Audio reported a study of viewers who watch hours and hours of home shopping channels. The study determined that the majority of people who call in and purchase items are regular viewers, many of them elderly shut-ins who tend to think of the television hosts as friends, and the show as a kind of virtual community. The study concluded that maybe, in a world with increasing personal disconnection, the only place where the most lonely of our society can find a place to belong is as a "member" of a club where the key requirement is to buy things. As William Dyrness has written, "the Freedom to be left alone has become the curse of being alone."[4] With rampant individualism, we have become a country of people who live out our existence in large part alone. This is a critical issue and backdrop as we consider the "why" question of human life.

A biologist friend said that science has one clear and consistent answer to the purpose of life. If you ask, Why do mosquitoes, and elephants, and humpback whales, and humans exist? the only answer from science is: To make more mosquitoes, elephants, humpback whales, and humans. He even told me of two species of insects, cicadas and mayflies, both of which live as adults for a very brief time, literally only enough time to mate and die. So, why do cicadas and mayflies and mosquitoes exist? All science can tell us is: To make more of the little buggers. And indeed, in the Scriptures, God commands that all the creatures of the world multiply and fill the earth.

But when we come to the Genesis account of human creation, an interesting twist occurs. Not only is the human the only creation that is very good, but the human is the only creature that is made in the image of God. And here in the concept of the image of God is the key to being human.

Usually when people refer to humans as made in the image of God, they assume that this means that humans are similar to God in certain qualities. That is, that we have the ability to make moral choices, or have rationality, the capacity to love, or a soul that can exist after death. But if we look at Genesis and compare it to other literature from the ancient Near East, we find a more consistent idea. In the cultures surrounding Israel, the image of a ruler was considered to have the authority of the ruler. Indeed, a conquering king would send his representative bearing his image (such as a statue or an engraving) into the outlying areas to proclaim his authority and exercise the rule of the new king. The image of the king (and the bearer of it) was believed to have the same power and authority as the king himself. The image-bearer was the ruler's representative. In Genesis, we see a similar function. Humans are made in the image of God and are charged with "exercising dominion," that is, being God's representative in a way that reflects God's character. That humans are made in the image of God means that whether we want to be or not, we are God's means for revealing himself in the world. Which of course raises two questions:

1. What does God "look" like?
2. How do we become like God so that we can image him accurately?

To understand this we will take a look backward to the theology of John Calvin. From him, we find a neglected description of the truly divine life-transformation built upon the concept of "mystical union" and experienced most profoundly in a most extraordinary ordinary place: the church.

Bringing Sanctification and Spirituality Together

> For those whom he foreknew he also predestined to be conformed to the image of his Son, in order that he might be the firstborn within a large family.
>
> Romans 8:29

God's divine intention is not, as we so often declare, to save people from their sins. At least it's not the ultimate intention. God's purpose in election is that we'll become like Christ. And not just you or me, but all of us, so that Christ might be the firstborn within a large family. The purpose of election is to have a whole family of the human family look like our big brother (who looks like our heavenly Father). God's intention from the beginning of time was that every human would look, in character, like Jesus.

This being the case, the divine intention for our churches is to be a community of conformity, transforming all people into the image of Christ. I often tell my church, "The purpose of San Clemente Presbyterian Church is to ensure that all people who come in here alienated from God find a relationship with God, take on the very character of God, and eventually look like God."

But how does that happen?

Certainly it begins in faith. As we trust in Christ as Savior and Lord, not only are we reconciled to God in justification, but we begin the process of sanctification, or becoming like Jesus (1 Cor. 6:11; 1 Peter 1:2). But how do we, who are saved by grace through faith and not because of any merit or improvement within us (Eph. 2:8–9; Titus 3:5), begin to truly change?

Historically, John Calvin gave the most comprehensive answer to that question. While many people think of Calvin as a great systematic theologian, he thought of his work as far more practical,[5] and of himself as a pastor less interested in "speculative" philosophical arguments than in what "moves the will" to respond to God's mercy in Jesus Christ and to grow in an ever deepening and life-transforming relationship with him.[6]

> My purpose was solely to transmit to certain rudiments by which those who are touched with any zeal for religion might be shaped to true godliness.[7]

For Calvin, this godly "shaping" was the focal point of his efforts, and anything that thwarted God's transforming work was to be opposed. Throughout his writings, Calvin has two foes, two groups of people whose ideas, Calvin believed, trapped people in a pattern of belief and action that would not bring change. Those two groups are specifically the "papists" and the "sophists," or, as I will refer to them, "the mimics" and the "exhorters."

Mocking the Mimics and Tossing Away the Trendy Jewelry

The first target of Calvin's polemic is the "papists" or Roman Catholics of his day. As one who was raised Catholic, I am always deeply uncomfortable with the harsh language of the Reformers toward the Catholicism of their day. But as Calvin aims his fiery invective at the dominant sixteenth-century church, we find very relevant warnings toward many facets of popular Christianity (especially Protestant Christianity!) today.

Unless you were locked away in the Amazon jungle the last few years, you probably knew that there was a bit of a trend of kids, particularly, and others wearing bracelets that read, "WWJD." The initials stood for a question that the one wearing pledged to ask in every circumstance of life: "What Would Jesus Do?"

That phrase was inspired by a late-nineteenth-century book by Charles Sheldon called *In His Steps*. The great irony is that today Sheldon would probably be considered to hold a more "liberal" or "social gospel" view of Christianity than most of the bracelet-wearing conservative Christians would be comfortable with.

Charles Sheldon's intention was to see the wealthy, upper-class industrialists of his day take seriously the commands of the gospel to care for the poor and disenfranchised of society. In Sheldon's story, a pastor who is busy working on his sermon in his study is interrupted by a vagrant's knock on the door. The pastor kindly but firmly sends him away, but the next day in the middle of his sermon, the guy shows up again and this time launches into a monologue in the middle of church. The vagrant asks, "What would Jesus do if he was here?" The pastor is so struck by the conviction of this man that he goes home thinking about it.

The man dies during the week, and the pastor is then inspired to preach a sermon the next week challenging his congregation to follow the vagrant's message. "If Jesus was here what would he do? Do not give any thought to the consequence and just do it." The book tells of a story of a town being virtually transformed. Homeless people are fed and given clothes, alcohol is dumped out all over the streets, and the town becomes a seemingly idyllic place to live. All because people decided to mimic whatever they thought Jesus would do in a given situation.

Fast-forward a century later, and you've got people with the same bracelet on but with different intentions. "What would Jesus do?" is not a rallying cry to social action, but instead a way to reinforce personal morals. It is a reminder to teenagers to think before they get into compromising situations at a party or in the backseat of a car.

Two centuries, two different moral emphases, but one message based on one assumption: that the model of Jesus (at least what we assume is the model of Jesus—we are asking a hypothetical question) will transform people as they seek to follow "in his steps."

Like many pastors, I have looked favorably upon the well-intentioned young people wearing their WWJD bracelets, and I have appreciated and even referenced Sheldon's book in sermons. But does wearing a bracelet, asking a question, or even trying to "imitate" a hypothetical Jesus really bring change? Pretty unlikely. And even more unlikely as it may sound, Calvin's argument against the "papists" is pretty applicable to all of us who believe change comes through copying Jesus.

In his discussion of sanctification, Calvin nuances the language of Matthew 16:24, where Jesus invites all who would be his disciples to "take up their cross and follow [him]."[8] He makes a distinction between "imitation of Christ" as following in faith and the popular understanding of imitation as mindlessly following the pattern of Jesus in life. We are to be "imitators, not apes,"[9] he says.

What does that mean? He believed that the significant problem with the Catholic faith in his day was the number of rituals that were followed to the letter mindlessly. Jesus was celibate, so all clergy were to be celibate. Jesus fasted, so Christians were to fast. Jesus fasted for forty days, so Lent would be forty days, and so on. Today, Calvin would be critical of those who, whenever they hear Handel's *Messiah,* just stand up and don't know why, who hang onto tradition for tradition's sake, or who believe that wearing a bracelet or copying Jesus without an internal change of heart will bring a transformation of life. No matter how well-intentioned, if it is mindless copying, it is unfruitful aping.

My friend Mark tells a story of when he was student at Harvard. A group of his friends went on a weekend retreat with Catholic spiritual writer Henri Nouwen. The students, all of them Protestants, were so deeply moved by Father Nouwen's prayerful example that a number of them began to imitate his prayers. The next week at their regular campus fellowship meeting, Mark noticed that a number of them were ending their verbal prayers with the phrase, "Lord, be with us now and in the hour of our dess." The hour of our dess? Mark wondered, What is dess? One of the students, answered, "Oh, we learned that from listening to Henri. That's how he ends his prayers. We think it means the moments of anguish, toil, and trial. It's a wonderful phrase, the way Henry prays it. It gives you peace to know that God will be with you in your dess."

But Mark, being curious and also quite good at languages, started thinking, Dess? Is that German? He tried to look it up, to no avail. And then one day he heard Henri pray aloud and realized that because Henri's native language was Dutch, his deeply accented prayer was "Be with us now and in the hour of our death," the final phrase to the Catholic prayer "the Hail Mary."

Those well-intentioned students didn't understand the word. They heard, but they merely mimicked their teacher in order to try to grow spiritually. Calvin would say that this is aping and that it won't bring lasting change.

Exposing the Exhorters: Turning off the Infomercial

The second teachers that Calvin criticized were the sophists.[10] The sophists were moral philosophers who wanted to appeal to reason, who believed that nature itself would point the way, that a rational, logical person will be led into the way of morals and will grow to become a better person through it.[11] I'm not sure if we have any sophists today; I don't remember seeing an ad for the Sophist Society meeting together. But in our society these are the self-help gurus and motivational moralists. With all due respect, Calvin may indeed consider Dr. Laura, Dr. Phil, or Tony Robbins a sophist. They can nag us, encourage us, instruct us, and motivate us, but all they can really do is talk to us. They don't, in themselves, have any power to change us.

According to Calvin, the sophists "set up reason alone as the ruling principle in man."[12] They use data and "appeals to nature"; they use "facts" and exhortation. But does it bring change?

I remember, from a speech communication class in college, examining the effectiveness of different forms of persuasion. In one study, researchers tested the effects of blunt confrontational information for persuading people with bad dental hygiene habits to brush their teeth more regularly. The subjects were shown pictures of rotting teeth and exhorted to avoid this fate at all costs. Sure enough, the participants in the study went home and brushed really, really hard that night and for maybe a night after. But soon enough they resumed their previous habits. Graphic exhortation has no lasting value in and of itself to bring enduring change.

While I was working on this book, I sat in a coffee shop shortly after New Year's Day listening to two men talk about their resolutions to lose weight. Both of them affirmed that they were ready to try a strict low-carbohydrate diet. They had lots of information, they understood the ins and outs of ketosis and metabolism, of blood sugar and high-protein foods. But when the waitress arrived to take their breakfast order, I heard one of them say, "Oh well, I'll still have the French toast."

What is true for dental hygiene and diets is even more true for holiness and life-transformation. While the philosophers and the sophists speak loftily about changed lives and moral virtues, Calvin is following Paul, who wrote, "I can will what is right, but I cannot do it. For I do not do the good I want, but the evil I do not want is what I do" (Rom. 7:18b–19). Reason, rational logic, and exhortation, while seemingly admirable, ultimately fail because reason in and of itself has no power to change the heart. The sophists can exhort, but without true knowledge of God, they can't arouse change.[13] For that, only true and sound biblical teaching, enlivened by the Holy Spirit, will suffice.

> We have given the first place to the doctrine in which our religion is contained, since our salvation begins with it. But, it must enter our hearts and pass along to our daily living, and so transform us into itself that it may not be unfruitful for us . . . [The Gospel's] efficacy ought to penetrate the inmost affections of the heart, take its seat in the soul and affect the whole man a hundred times more deeply than the cold exhortations of the philosophers![14]

From Calvin we learn that the way of reason, self-help, and moralism is the most dangerous way of thinking. It is the trap of believing that you can reason your way to what is right, that you can simply, in Jiminy Cricket fashion, "Let your conscience be your guide." It's the good moral person who will not yield to Christ because he or she steadfastly claims to be good enough without him. If any of us think that through common sense, determination, sheer willpower, exhortation, or some self-improvement plan, we can change ourselves for good, we're far away from conformity with Christ. Without having our hearts aroused by the Spirit, the exhortations of the infomercialists will eventually fail and only frustrate.

But for Calvin, the monumental failure of both the papists' and the sophists' teaching to bring change is that both rely on approaches *that are completely devoid of relationship*. While these teachers know "droplets of truth,"[15] they do not know God's "fatherly favor in our behalf in which salvation consists."[16] They are ignorant of the relational dynamic of sanctification.

Calvin's argument against the papists and the sophists sets the stage for better understanding his discussion for what does bring change in the Christian life. In these arguments, Calvin hammers home that God's predestined intention for humanity is that we would be conformed in character to be like Jesus. Neither the way of mimicry nor that of exhortation will do. But, we ask, if my transformation does not come through mimicking Christ with my body and always trying to "do the right thing" and if it's not about thinking and acting reasonable, then what is it about?

It's about union.

Mystical Union, Transformation, and a Wedding Day

Sanctification is not mindless mimicry of even ethical behavior nor rational and reasonable thinking, but "conformity with Christ,"[17] which comes about only as a person is "awakened," "quickened," or "aroused" in his or her heart to desire God, is regenerated by the Holy Spirit in order for the mind to see the truth without the distortion of fallenness, and is led into a relationship with Christ that serves as the channel for ongoing change. It is this union—and only this union—of Christ with the believer that brings real, godly transformation of life.[18] Listen to Calvin's own words here:

> Christ is not outside us but dwells within us. Not only does he cleave to us by an indivisible bond of fellowship, but with a wonderful communion, day by day, he grows more and more into one body with us until he becomes completely one with us.[19]

For Calvin and those who followed his theological lead, sanctification of a believer comes *only* through union with Christ by the Holy Spirit.[20] Union given graciously as a gift by God *is* justification.[21] And union, sustained graciously by God, is the empowering source for the Christian life of "repentance" expressed in "following Christ."[22]

This point is crucial. While this language often makes us nervous,[23] at the very center of Calvin's theology and practical instruction is this "mystical union" of Christ with the believer. (Some have even argued that it could be the elusive "central dogma" of Calvin's thought.)[24] Since both salvation and transformation come through the mystical union of the believer with Christ, Christianity is best understood as a *relational* life that progresses in greater trust and devotion (relationship to God) and more consistent expression and transformed living (relationship to other people).[25] The believer brought into union with Christ is empowered by the Holy Spirit through that union for fulfilling the purposes of human existence.

> Let us know the unity that we have with our Lord Jesus Christ; to wit, that he wills to have a common life with us, and that what he has should be ours: Nay, that he even wishes to dwell in us, not in imagination, but in effect, not in earthly fashion but spiritually; and that whatever may befall, he so labours by the virtue of his Holy Spirit that we are united with him more closely than are the limbs of his body.[26]

Here Calvin uses a metaphor from which he draws frequently, that of limbs to the body, or even more often, "members" to the "head." This is not to imply a mixing of substance but is to demonstrate the degree of intimacy and the certainty of the enduring power of the union.[27] But an even more fundamental image is the marriage analogy that describes the union between Christ and believers in Ephesians 5.

In his commentary on Ephesians 5:29, Calvin says, "That unity which belongs to marriage is declared to exist between himself and the church. This is a remarkable passage on the mysterious intercourse which we have with Christ." Here we have something foundational for Calvin's use of mystical union: the "mystery" of how a "one flesh" union with Christ changes the believer into conformity with Christ.[28] In commenting on Ephesians 5:32, Calvin says that the "great mystery" that cannot be fully understood (especially by skeptics) is that by this union "Christ breathes into the Church his life and power." "For here [in the union], the infinite power of the Divine Spirit is exerted."[29] The Spirit joins the believer with Christ in the same way that a husband is joined with his wife, not in confusion of identity but by a bond of the Holy Spirit.[30]

This is the true power of the gospel: Christ enters into us, joins himself to us, and changes us into his image. The power of Christianity is built around the reality of union. And not just a union where Christ joins himself to us, but a union where through the relationship we grow to become more and more like the one to whom we are joined. It's like a wedding and marriage.

The whole point of marriage is not the wedding day. One of the most frustrating parts of being a pastor is trying to prepare couples for a marriage while they are planning a wedding. They are always far more excited about the big day with family, friends, good food, presents, a wedding night, and a honeymoon than they are talking about the next forty or fifty years of living together as one flesh. Understandably, they are more interested in the wedding than in the marriage, but as a pastor, I try to say as gently as possible, "It ain't about the day."

It could rain on your wedding day; the flower girl could get sick on your dress, the photographer could forget to put film in the camera, it could be a horrible day, but what really matters (though I do want it to be a nice day, really) is not the day, but the life that follows the day. How many beautiful weddings have we seen? Remember the fairy-tale wedding of Princess Diana and Prince Charles? Well, the marriage certainly wasn't.

So often as Christians we focus on the "wedding day" of our salvation—the day a person begins a relationship with Christ. And yes, that is an exciting day. Salvation comes to the person, and the Spirit takes up residence in the center of that person's being. But what about the next day and the day after that?

When Calvin comments on Ephesians 5, he doesn't give a sermon on "submission" or family relationships; he instead spends the entire passage talking about the intimacy of how Christ weds himself to us and how we are to be cleaved. The language comes right out of Genesis—that when we become believers, we are cleaved to Christ. And that literally we're one flesh with Christ. And that we're transformed through living with Christ. Believers and Jesus are to become like an old married couple who have stared at each other every morning over oatmeal for so long that they begin to look alike.

He offers an important description (and let me clarify with comments along the way):

> That joining together of head and members [Christ is the head, we're the members], that indwelling of Christ in our hearts. In short, that mystical union, [this is wedding language,—technically, this is wedding-

> *night* language] are accorded by us the highest degree of importance, so that Christ, having been made ours, *makes us sharers with him in the gifts with which he has been endowed*.

Do you now recognize what Calvin is teaching here? He's saying that everything that Christ has becomes yours, and everything that is yours becomes Christ's. The way the bank account becomes one in a marriage. The way the property becomes joint. The way in which at that moment when I officiate a wedding I tell couples that their lives are joined together in such a way that it will take an act of God and the state of California to separate them—and I also tell them, God will be more disappointed and the state will be more annoying if you do. Let's finish the quote:

> We do not, therefore, contemplate him outside ourselves from afar in order that his righteousness may be imputed to us, *but because we put on Christ and are engrafted into his body. In short, because he deigns to make us one with him* [emphasis mine].[31]

Here, Calvin pulls together a clothing metaphor ("put on Christ"), an anatomical metaphor ("head to members"), and union language ("mystical union") in what is probably the definitive passage for simultaneously tying together his notion of "union" as *both* justification and sanctification.[32] So union with Christ is both the foundation of "conformity with Christ" and, in a progressive way, the means to "conformity with Christ" as that union deepens.[33]

It was important to Calvin that this union with Christ was not reserved for "mystics" alone, but involved participation in the ascended life of Christ for all believers.[34] Indeed, the effectual transformation comes as the believer is *empowered* by the union with Christ,[35] specifically, and as we shall see, most importantly for this discussion, through the Lord's Supper.

What does Christ do that's different? What do we have in the gospel that's different from aping, moral mimicry, or nagging rationality? God himself enters our hearts, grows within us, and changes us from the inside out. The Christian life is not primarily one of showing people what Jesus would do or getting a 100 percent grade on a theological test. While it certainly includes both ethics and doctrine, it recognizes that mind and living begin with the genuine, renewed, and transformed heart that only Christ can bring. It begins by saying yes to him and allowing his Spirit to live in us. And as his Spirit lives in us and grows in us, we begin to change.

What is the difference between true faith and the mimics and the exhorters? No matter how well-intentioned we are, no matter how great it is to look at that bracelet on my wrist and or to try to live a reasonable life, if Jesus isn't in us—joined to us—then it is a waste of time.

For Calvin, that's the important part of Christianity. What makes Christianity different—how we'll be transformed—is not based upon all the great preachers and all the great moral and ethical teaching, but upon God himself entering within us and transforming us. The process of *how* God does that is what we need to explore next. It is a mystery, indeed. But we shouldn't shy away from trying to understand it and then cultivate it. As Stanley Hauerwas has written,

> the problem does not focus so much on the notion of "mystical union" with Christ, but rather on the inability to characterize the human side of that union. Protestant theology has resisted spelling out the union for fear that any attempts to explain or make this union intelligible in terms of a concrete view of the self would make the mystery of grace disappear in some reductionist form of empirical psychology. It may well be that grace is a mystery, but *mystery is hardly preserved by resisting any attempt to understand the nature of the self that is graced* [emphasis mine].[36]

Understanding "the nature of the self that is graced" is indeed our endeavor, but in order to do that, we need a more thorough understanding of the Divine Self that does the gracing. So, next we turn our attention to the Trinity.

4

The Transforming Communion

Some years ago, when I was an associate pastor, a woman walked in my office and sat down in front of me.

"How can I help you?" I began.

"I'd like you to lead me to Christ."

"Excuse me?"

"I'd like to become a Christian, and I'd like you to baptize me."

Huh? [You see, even as a pastor, I don't have a conversation like this very often.] "Aren't I at least supposed to tell you a couple of spiritual laws or something? Aren't I supposed to talk you into this?"

"No. No. I've come to have you do this." "Okay," I said "I guarantee you won't get out the door before we pray for you to receive Christ, and we will schedule your baptism, but I have to know the story here."

And she told me this story:

A year or so earlier she had come to the young adult fellowship group that I led. "I thought the class was great," she said. "I got to know these wonderful people. I loved the way they interacted with one another and cared for one another. I knew they had something that I didn't have.

"You see, I did not grow up in a religious home; I've wandered through lots of different things, just searching and struggling at times. When I came to the fellowship group, I decided that whatever they had, I really wanted. But as you taught about Jesus, I just had too many intellectual questions.

"Ultimately," she said, "I decided that I needed to leave the fellowship, because at the core of your beliefs was the conviction that Jesus was God, and I just didn't believe it. A spiritual teacher or a prophet maybe, but not God.

"So I continued to search. But, after leaving the fellowship I was so lonely that I started to ask myself why I was having trouble making relationships. I came to admit that my biggest problems stemmed from growing up in an alcoholic home. So I joined a 12-step group for adult children of alcoholics.

"I tried to seek a Higher Power, even though I didn't know who that was. As I prayed and experienced a sense of peace, I wanted to know my Higher Power better, so—I don't really know why—but I picked up a Bible that I had had when I was in your class and I started reading it. And as I read, I recognized my Higher Power right there in the Gospels. All of a sudden I realized that the Jesus on that page was the same one that you were talking about, the same one that was at the core of your fellowship and was the one I had been praying to as a Higher Power. And so I decided that I would come and ask you help me become a Christian."

I said, "What happened to your intellectual problems?" She said, "They all went away. Jesus was the only one who made sense. And only the Trinity that you Christians believe in could make sense of the fact that I had experienced the same love in your fellowship, the same joy in prayer, and the same truth in the word in front of me. That had to be the one God, that's the one that I want to follow." It was probably the first time in my life I met someone who became a trinitarian before becoming a Christian.

In this chapter we are going to explore the doctrine of the Trinity so that we can ultimately understand this truth: *Christian transformation comes through the pattern, the personal relationship, and the power of God to the believer found in Jesus Christ through the Spirit experienced within the community.*

From the Communion of the Trinity to a Community of Transformation

> The transfiguration of bodiliness is the goal . . . Faith as understanding is the beginning; the lived gestalt of faith is the purposed end.[1]

From Calvin we learned that God's purpose from the beginning of time was the transformation of human beings into the character of Jesus. In this chapter we will see how that "transfiguration of bodiliness" (to use Jürgen Moltmann's phrase in the quote above) is rooted in the very being of the Triune God. We will see how the trinitarian life of God becomes for us the life of the Spirit that we enjoy as believers and that transforms our communal life as the body of Christ in the world. This transforming communion is founded on the doctrine of the Trinity and is expressed in the life of the church.

In order to live out this transforming communion, in the remainder of the chapters of this book we will take up the central activities of the church as worship, word, and witness. Each of these activities will be recast as intentional expressions of the trinitarian life that transforms us into the incarnated Trinity, Jesus Christ. But first, we need to get a clear "picture" of the Trinity.

In the fifteenth-century icon *The Holy Trinity,* painted by Andrei Rublev,[2] three divine figures gather around a common table, each holding a staff in his left hand, each with his head gently inclined toward the others, right hands pointing to a chalice filled with wine at the center of the table. Unlike so many icons where the Spirit is portrayed as a dove or a light, the Trinity is depicted as three persons, all equally sharing rule (symbolized by their staffs), in loving communion (symbolized by the inclined heads), and joined together by a common table and a common cup. The table symbolizes the fellowship and hospitality they share and, ultimately, offer. The cup symbolizes the "sorrows" and "suffering" that they share and offer with the haunting words of Jesus to his disciples: "Are you able to drink the cup that I drink?"[3] Because of the two-dimensional nature of the icon, the prayerful believer finds himself or herself as the fourth person seated at the table, drawn into the fellowship and intimacy of the Persons, as well as the cup of sacrificial love they drink.

This icon serves as an evocative starting point. The Godhead as Persons, equally sharing rule, equally involved in redemptive suffering for the world, equally and intimately united to each other, invite the believer into their fellowship of intimacy and suffering love. The believer finding the comfort of fellowship with the Triune

God becomes a partner in comforting ministry (2 Cor. 1:3–7). It is a communion that is grounded in love, expressed in mutuality, intimacy, and hospitality, and then is demonstrated in its ministry in the world.

If our churches are going to form exceptional lives that reflect this Triune God, then we must ensure that our church practices intentionally reflect this Triune God. But before we can undertake that task, we will first devote this chapter to truly understanding what philosophers call the ontological reality of the Trinity: that is, the way that God is in God's being. The way God really is.

God Is a Covenant Group

Whenever one looks in the Bible for the doctrine of the Trinity, they will inevitably have a hard time finding it. Indeed, you can't even look up the word *Trinity* in a concordance, because the word itself never appears in the Bible. And since the Bible isn't a textbook on theology, you won't even find

I. God
  A. Definition of
    i. Trinity

The Bible is the divinely inspired record or revelation of God's encounter with humanity and humanity's response. It is written in narrative form, and theological descriptions like the Trinity have to be gleaned from several different, but not explicit texts.

Some key passages:

- The Great Commission of Matthew 28:19 frames the entire Christian endeavor in trinitarian terms. "Go therefore and make disciples of all nations, baptizing them in the name of the Father and of the Son and of the Holy Spirit . . ."
- In 1 Peter 1, we have a description of Christians as those "who have been chosen and destined by God the Father and sanctified by the Spirit to be obedient to Jesus Christ . . ."

- Then, in Ephesians 2:18, we have a wonderful description of the way in which Christ is bringing reconciliation to both Jews and Gentiles: "for through him both of us have access in one Spirit to the Father."
- Finally, in 2 Corinthians 13:13, we receive the benediction: "The grace of the Lord Jesus Christ, the love of God, and the communion of the Holy Spirit be with all of you."

The Trinity in Recent Theology

The modern resurgence of theological emphasis on the Trinity is undoubtedly traced back to volume 1 of Karl Barth's *Church Dogmatics.*[4] Barth placed the doctrine of the Trinity in a place of prominence in his system, and, as such, it is the first principle from which all Christian theology flows. The result has been no shortage of studies about the Trinity, but unfortunately, precious little of that discussion has been of help to everyday Christians and busy pastors trying to shape churches and encourage Christian faithfulness. As Dorothy L. Sayers has said, to the average churchgoer,

> the Father is incomprehensible, the Son is incomprehensible, and the whole thing is incomprehensible. Something put in by theologians to make it more difficult—nothing to do with daily life or ethics.[5]

Lately, however, a number of recent scholarly works have focused on the Trinity as the theological framework of the church.[6] In a statement that is entirely consistent with what we have learned already from Calvin's view of the Christian life as a relational life,[7] Catherine Mowry LaCugna offers:

> The doctrine of the Trinity is ultimately a practical doctrine with radical consequences for Christian life. . . . [The very purpose of the Christian life] is to participate in the life of God through Jesus Christ in the Spirit. . . . Divine life is therefore also *our* life. The heart of the Christian life is to be united with the God of Jesus Christ by means of communion with each other. The doctrine of

the Trinity is ultimately therefore a teaching not about the abstract nature of God, nor about God in isolation from everything other than God, but a teaching about God's life with us and our life with each other.[8]

In many ways, then, the doctrine of the Trinity leads us to see that life is in its essence a relationship. While so many in our society celebrate the significance of the solitary individual, the truth is that humans are, by nature and design, deeply dependent upon one another. Just watch a baby who cries to nurse even after he has been weaned, a child who loves exploring the world until her parents are out of sight and then comes running back, a teenager who spends all night sending "instant messages" on the Internet to friends, adults who rearrange successful lives to settle down and start a family, and so on. No matter the life stage, we are always struggling and seeking relationships. The doctrine of the Trinity reminds us that the God who made us in his image considered his own human creation "not good" until he created a second one for relationship (Gen. 1:27). The doctrine of the Trinity teaches us that since God is a relationship, then we "image" God only in relationship.

In the Beginning: *Communion?*

To clearly understand what this means to us, we have to enter a pretty technical debate. Ever since the Council of Chalcedon in 381 A.D., one of the key questions about God has been about the *priority* of God's nature. Is God first and foremost *the unity* of trinitarian essence or the *plurality* of the trinitarian persons?

The Western tradition (in contrast to Eastern Orthodox thought) since Augustine has argued consistently for the unity of God's essence (the Latin word *substantia)* constituted as three divine persons (Latin, *personae)*. This perspective developed into the "psychological analogy" drawn between the immanent Trinity and the human mind.[9]

For the past generation, however, there has been a resurgence in the influence of Eastern scholarship that was based more on the early writings of the Cappadocian fathers who preferred a more "social analogy."[10] In a nutshell, the debate boils down to this question: Is God's essence *lordship* or *love*? Of course, we cannot separate the two, but what is primary about the nature of God? Is it that there is one God who is "the LORD alone" (Deut. 6:4), or is it that "God is love"? (1 John 4:8).[11] This debate has raged in a number of circles (and is certainly more technical than simply a question about whether the Old Testament or the New Testament views of God take priority), but the debate begins to be resolved through seeing the interrelatedness of each of the divine persons in every divine act.

Perichoresis: All of God in Every Divine Act

In recent gatherings in my denomination, there have been frequent moves to rewrite the doxology in less overtly masculine language for the Trinity. So instead of praising "Father, Son, and Holy Ghost," from whom all blessings flow, the well-intentioned singers praise "Creator, Christ, and Holy Ghost." The assumption is that God the Father is equivalent to God the Creator and that the Son alone is the Christ, and so on.

At first glance it seems a rather benign way of using inclusive language and covering all the bases. But careful review raises some potential problems far more distressing than inclusive language for God (as sensitive as I am about wanting to eliminate stumbling blocks for worshipers).

It's worth reexamining the language. Did God the Father create alone? Genesis says that God created through the Spirit, and John says that the Son, or Logos, was present. (Gen. 1:1, 2:7; John 1:3). What about in salvation? Jesus Christ saves, but only as he is resurrected by the Father and commits his spirit to the Father and receives the Holy Spirit (Eph. 2:4–6; Acts 2:33–34). And what about the Spirit's work of sanctification? We're sanctified by the Spirit of Jesus through the work of God sustaining us (1 Cor. 6:11; Rom. 8:28–39).

So the doctrine of the Trinity requires that while certain aspects of salvation are attributed to one person of the Trinity, in fact, every divine act involves the entire Trinity operating interdependently. Therefore, both the sociality of the persons of the Trinity and the unity of Godhead are maintained by keeping the focus on God's actions.

Beth and I are committed to parenting our two children with one voice. That is, we know that they will be more secure and more apt to heed our desires for them if we first agree on everything that we are asking of them. Are we going to limit TV? Are we going to set new bedtimes or expectations for when homework is done? Then we had better be clear between the two of us before we tell the kids. But sometimes one of us has to make a decision without consulting the other. Whenever that occurs, the parent who did not make the decision always supports the decision made. *Always*. (Oh, we may "discuss" it later, but in front of the kids, we are one voice.) If you ask our kids who made the rule or decision, they will always say, "BOTH of them did. Our parents did." One of us may have implemented it, but both of us decided it. In a similar way, no matter who implements an act of God, all of God acted.

Where this becomes most critical is in understanding how we humans come to know anything or anyone. Through the actions of people around us, responding to us, we come to know both them and ourselves. When teachers tell us we are smart, or friends laugh at our jokes, or a parent smiles at us, we know something about their feelings or opinions as well as about our character or personality. Relational knowledge is learned through the actions of people in relationship to us.

In the same way that humans learn who they are through their encounter with other humans, the personal encounter with God through a saving relationship ultimately leads to our understanding of who God is. God, as God acts in Jesus through the Spirit, is revealed to us as a Trinity.[12] When we come to faith, we experience God coming to us as triune: a loving Father who reaches out to us, a Savior Son who dies for us, and a transforming Spirit who enables us to believe. We discover in the actions of God through each Person the unity of God that is in all.[13] This experience of the interrelatedness of the persons of the Trinity in every divine act is the classical concept of perichoresis, defined as "the passing into one another of the divine persons."[14]

> Suppose . . . there are disembodied agents who are also without sin, each defining its own identity in genuine otherness, each losing itself

> in common enterprise pursued without jealousy or conflict, so at one that each was in all. . . . God exists three-personedly, but none of those three persons have independent existence, for they are what they are in relation, so that God is what God is in this interrelatedness.[15]

This "interrelated" God is experienced in the *work* of God, which comes to us in our encounter with God.[16] Like the way that a musical trio needs each voice singing each distinctive part to produce a song as it is written, each Person of the Trinity is both distinct and necessary, interrelated and yet not confused.

Think back to the story about the woman who discovered Christ in the unity of her experiences within a Christian fellowship, in her Bible reading, and in praying to her Higher Power. What is most significant about this illustration is that the young woman's encounter with God was a result of both her *personal experience* through her psychological need and her connection of that personal experience to the *social relationships* with Christians in our adult fellowship. The friendships with Christians and the teaching of the Scriptures came together as she began to humbly pray for help. Through *encounter* and *relationship* she discovered the unity of God in the very *diversity of revelation*. The ministry of God in her life as both the comforting Spirit and the revealed Word, Jesus Christ, led her to trust the Triune God. I am convinced that this woman would agree with Gregory of Nazianzus who wrote of the Godhead so "perichoretically united" as like *three* suns shining to form *one* beam.[17]

> When we think of three so united in purpose and actuality, beyond all discord, when we think of one God so rich in love, the questions of whether there are three individuals or one melt away. Not three isolated individuals; not one without internal distinction. Each is full selfhood precisely in community, each one most itself in its threeness.[18]

So, How Do We Get to Know the "Real" God?

If our encounter of God leads to experiencing God as triune, then the expected questions are, "But how do we know who God is? How can we be sure that we are not just perceiving what we want to perceive or even projecting onto God our ideas about God? How do we come to know the very character of God?"

If you and I were to meet in an airport somewhere and strike up a conversation, before long I would be proudly taking out pictures of my wife and kids. If you said to me, "Tell me about your wife," I wouldn't need to speak of her beauty (it would be obvious from the picture!), but I would probably start telling you stories of how she loves people and laughs easily and is a caring mother and great listener. But what if you interrupted me and said, "Well, that's how she *acts,* but tell me about who she *is!*"? Frankly, I'd be a bit stumped. You see, I have known Beth for half of my adult life and probably know her better than any person on earth, but it is very difficult to describe the inner core of a person, the whole true character and being of a person. I could spend hours telling you about her and still not adequately and completely describe her.

Just think how difficult that is to do with God. But there is a theological rule that while humans sometimes act in ways that are contradictory to their character, God always acts as God is.[19] That is, the God who is revealed through his saving work is necessarily identical to the being of God in himself (whether he is saving us or not). If God is truly the God of Jesus Christ, then that is what he is like eternally. In the ministry of Jesus, the revelation of the character of God and the saving communion are both made known.[20]

All of this now leads us to consider ourselves. If God is known only through God's actions, then how is God known today? There aren't many burning bushes, and Jesus died on the cross a long time ago. How does God act in showing his character today? Here is the sobering answer: Through the church. Christ acts through his body.

In 1 Corinthians 3:16, Paul asks, "Do you not know that you are God's temple and that God's Spirit dwells in you?" While this verse is often interpreted to mean that God dwells in each individual Christian, it is clearly speaking to the corporate body, the church. The church replaces the temple as the dwelling place of God on earth. Further, in 1 Corinthians 12 and also in Ephesians 3–4, Paul refers to the community as Christ's body that together reveals or glorifies God. God reveals himself through the church. This led Dietrich Bonhoeffer to call the church "Christ existing as community."[21]

If Christ is present today as the church, and the church is God's means of self-revelation to the world, then the church is called to live and act together in such a way as to demonstrate God's character. In other words, if God is as God acts, then the church should act as God is. The basis of Christian life together must be to reflect or embody the very actions and character of God.

Through God's saving act, we learn that God is one Lord, Father, Son, and Holy Spirit. We also come to understand that lordship is expressed into the world as sacrificial love. Through God's gracious ministry of loving rule, suffering love, revelatory redemption, and empowering transformation, we come to know God as triune and experience the nature of the communion of the Trinity as shared and sacrificial love.[22] Once we understand that, then we discover how we are to live.

What Does It Mean to Be God's Image?

In some sense, the starting point for discussing the nature of God depends upon one's pastoral aims. Is the purpose to defend the church from heresies of polytheism or pluralistic spiritualities? Then the nature of God as the one and only Lord must be asserted. But if the pastoral aim is to reveal the nature of God in his saving and life-transforming encounter with people (and then to determine our faithful response to God), the nature of God as loving relationship is most appropriate.

John Zizoulas traces the growth of the social analogy of the Trinity back to the patristic pastoral theologians. While the Greek academic doctors (Clement, Origen, et al.) wrestled with ontological monism in combating gnostic spiritualities of their day, the bishops of the period (Ignatius of Antioch, Irenaeus, and later Athanasius) "approached the being of God through the experience of the ecclesial community, of ecclesial being. This experience revealed something very important: the being of God could be known only through personal relationships and personal love, best expressed as communion . . . The being of God is a relational being: without the concept of communion it would not be possible to speak of God."[23]

Indeed, for these bishops, communion was an ontological category. That is, a relationship is not something that can be reduced to a smaller part, but either exists or not. When does someone become a father, a mother, a brother, a sister? When a relationship is "birthed." A man cannot be a father without having a son or daughter. In the same way, we don't have spouses or friends without someone to wed or befriend. A relationship is not reduced to the persons in the relationship but exists as an entity in itself. The Triune God is the same way. If we reduce God into three separate Gods, we have tri-theism (the belief in three Gods), but by holding to the belief that the essence of God is the love and relationship shared within the Trinity, then that shared love and relationship—that communion—is therefore the essence of God.[24]

In Rublev's *Holy Trinity*, the divine Persons gather at a table of shared communion, joined together by their shared ministry of sacrificial love as represented in the chalice of wine. The picture gives us a glimpse of who God is that is consistent with how God is revealed in the actions of Jesus Christ, simultaneously.[25]

We see that God is communion. We also see that the ministry of Jesus in the cross is the ministry of the Trinity inviting us into God's own communion of intimacy, where true personhood and eternal life is found and expressed. But with the invitation to fellowship with God also comes the invitation to share the ministry that flows to all people from that communion.

This understanding of God as Divine Communion leads us to better understand ourselves also. Since God, the Divine Person, is a communion, human personhood means "existing-in-relationship."[26] Most significantly, the goal of all human life is found in and only in the call to and continuance of a relationship with God. "To be a human is to be related to the Father through the Son and in the Spirit, and it is the character of Christian experience to realize that relationship."[27] Or, as Moltmann declares, the "history of salvation is the history of the eternally living and Triune God who draws us into and includes us in his eternal Triune life with all the fullness of its relationships."[28]

This is the place where the reader can sigh in relief. We are now back on familiar terrain. Jesus said, "This is eternal life, that they may know you, the only true God, and Jesus Christ whom you have sent" (John 17:3). To know God and Jesus—to have a relationship with them—is to have eternal life. But eternal life as God's intention for persons (indeed understood as true personhood) is always constituted by the call of God through other persons. Miroslav Volf reminds us that "without other human beings, even God cannot create a human being."[29]

So, all the more, Christian personhood is constituted through the invitation into relationship with God through other people. Salvation is always communicated through the instrumentality of the church, and the invitation to participate in the life of the Trinity presumes relationships with others.

In language that points us back to the picture of Rublev's icon, Volf reminds us that relationship with God is founded upon the gracious invitation to participate in God's eternal community.

> Because the Christian God is not a lonely God, but rather a communion of the three persons, faith leads human beings into the divine *communio*. One cannot, however, have a self-enclosed communion with the Triune God—a "foursome," as it were—for the Christian God is not a private deity. Communion with this God is at once also communion with those others who have entrusted themselves in faith to the same God. Hence one and the same act of faith places a person into a new relationship both with God and with all others who stand in communion with God.[30]

Salvation or eternal life is to join, as it were, the "table fellowship" of the Trinity that is depicted in Rublev's icon, and to be transformed by the love of the fellowship into the likeness of the divine Persons. Because the actions of the Trinity reveal the nature of God as communion, and because we find our own identity and salvation through that communion, *we have a vision for the life of the church that is directly grounded in the experience and reality of God.* We have been graciously received into the communion of the Triune God and experience the love of God in Jesus Christ through the Holy Spirit who is conforming us to Christ. Not only is God a Trinity through whom persons are defined, but Christian community is defined and given its normative example for living as the earthly depiction of the divine community.[31] As LaCugna has written, the "life of God is not something that belongs to God alone. *The trinitarian life is also our life.*"[32]

Exploring that trinitarian life is our next task.

5

Living the Trinity

> "Teacher, which commandment in the law is the greatest?" He said to him, "'You shall love the Lord your God with all your heart, and with all your soul, and with all your mind.' This is the greatest and first commandment. ***And a second is like it:*** 'You shall love your neighbor as yourself.' On these two commandments hang all the law and the prophets."
>
> Matthew 22:36–40

This statement (emphasis mine) is by far the most radical in this book. And for many of us, Matthew 22:39 is about the most difficult Bible verse to believe. While some academics trace the problem to a misunderstanding of the very nature of God in Augustinian theology, for most of us, the struggle was born from the messages of well-meaning evangelical teachers (most of whom had probably never read Augustine).[1] My own experience is probably a common one.

I'm a product of the success of mid-twentieth-century evangelicalism[2] that rightly restored and reignited the popular idea that God wants to save us from hell, but more than that, passionately desires to have "a personal relationship" with us. Having grown up as a Roman Catholic, my teenage struggles were not so much with belief as they were with commitment: the reframing of faith as a relationship with Christ, rather than an obligation to God requiring my devotion and discipline.

Unfortunately, what most of us heard in those kinds of messages is that we can have a personal *and private* relationship with Christ. I remember my youth leader giving an invitation and saying, "There is nothing to join, you don't have to be a church member. It's just about having a relationship with Jesus." And I wanted that. Not church, but Jesus. Shortly after I committed my life to following Christ, I bought a T-shirt that said "JC and me." It was my not-so-subtle way of sharing my faith, and it described my new-found belief perfectly. This wasn't my parents' religion, this wasn't about tradition or ritual, it was just about "JC and me"—a sentiment that always sounds good until you start reading the Bible.

What is the earliest result of the very first Christian sermon? Peter preached the gospel, and Acts 2:41–42 says, "So those who welcomed his message were baptized, and that day about three thousand persons were added. They devoted themselves to the apostles' teaching and fellowship, to the breaking of bread and the prayers." Not much "just JC and me" there. The earliest believers trust the good news about Jesus and join—through baptism—the fellowship of people who also trust this message.

Notice also that the first "spiritual disciplines" were all communal ones. They did not race home, have a personal quiet time, and give up smoking, but instead "devoted themselves" to "the apostles' teaching" (shared beliefs), "fellowship" (shared relationships), "breaking of bread" (shared meals), and "the prayers" (shared spiritual life), all expressed in a communal life together. Indeed the passage goes on (vv. 43–47) to demonstrate just how quickly and how completely the personal conversion experience reoriented a new convert's whole communal life.

> Awe came upon everyone, because many wonders and signs were being done by the apostles. All who believed were together and had all things in common; they would sell their possessions and goods and distribute the proceeds to all, as any had need. Day by day, as they spent much time together in the temple, they broke bread at home and ate their food with glad and generous hearts, praising God and having the goodwill of all the people. And day by day the Lord added to their number those who were being saved.

Try to find any instance in the Bible in which someone just "accepts Jesus" and then goes merrily on his or her own way. It just doesn't happen. Yet that is what so many of us do. We think that salvation consists of intellectual assent to the right statements and a desire to clean up one's act. Well-meaning Christians relegate the church to "support" and "assistance" for the individual journey of following Christ. Personally, it took nearly a decade of being a committed Christian before I realized how inextricable to Christian faith is the community of Christian people.

Indeed, what we could call an "unchurched Christian" today was considered in the first century to be a person "turned over to Satan."[3] 1 Peter 2:10 equates receiving God's mercy with being part of the people of God and *not* being part of the people of God with *not* receiving God's mercy. In words offered by Emil Brunner that should be emblazoned on a plaque on every pastor's desk:

> *The fellowship of Christians is just as much an end in itself as is their fellowship with Christ.* This quite unique meeting of the horizontal and the vertical is the consequence and the type of that communion which the father has with the Son "before the world was" (John 17:5, 24); in the supernatural life of the Christian communion is completed the revelation of the Triune God . . . the very being of God is agape—that love which the Son brings to mankind from the Father, and it is just this love which is the essence of the fellowship of those who belong to the *Ecclesia.*[4]

The love shared within the Trinity and brought into the world by Jesus is the very same merciful and gracious love that is meant to be shared, demonstrated, and offered to others in and through the church. To believe in the Trinity is to live the Trinity. To live the Trinity is to be part of God's relational-sacramental life.

Relational-Sacramental Life

> The history of salvation is the history of the eternally living and Triune God who draws us into and includes us in his eternal Triune life with all the fullness of its relationships.[5]

Since God's purpose for human beings is conformity with Christ (Rom. 8:29) who is the image of God—and since the image of God revealed by Christ is triune communion—spiritual formation in Christ will necessarily be what I am terming *relational-sacramental* in nature. That is, because God's essence is loving relationship, Christian maturity and growth will always entail growth in healthy and God-reminiscent relationships. At the same time, since God is known only through his self-revelation in Jesus within this world, mature Christian expression will result in human living that reveals the presence and character of God in everyday life. Let's look at the two dimensions of this spirituality separately before we try to pull them together.

"Relational": Perichoretic Living

> For Paul, the Gospel bound men and women to one another as well as to God. Acceptance by Christ necessitated acceptance of those whom he had already welcomed (Rom. 15:7). . . . Union in the Spirit involved union with one another for the Spirit was primarily a shared, not an individual experience.[6]

What I mean by living the Trinity as a "relational spirituality" is probably, by now, obvious. Since the very essence of the Trinity is the shared, interrelated (or *perichoretic*) communion of love between Father, Son, and Holy Spirit, then the "essence" of the church reflecting the Trinity is not some "other" substance but the unity its members' love for one another (John 13:34–35).[7] Through that love, the communion of the Trinity graciously granted to the believer is expressed. Indeed, the formation of that community is the "goal of God's life-giving Spirit in the world of nature and human beings."[8]

But the depths of that relational life are not as obvious. For if "God is what God is in interrelatedness,"[9] then human transformation is both dependent upon and realized in a similar interrelatedness. Humans are created physically through physical union, we grow in families through loving attachment, and we become spiritually mature through interdependent living. Human living in the image of God is perichoretic also. The mature Christian maintains his or her identity but his or her life and essence is subsumed within larger actions of God's actions within the Christian community.

This offers both good and sobering news to us as Christians. Romans 12:5 teaches us that "we, who are many, are one body in Christ, and *individually we are members one of another*" (emphasis mine). Our membership as Christians is not some organization, but to "one another," a phrase that shows up in Paul's writings more than three dozen times. Because of who we are in Christ, our life is one of deep "one another living": welcoming one another, greeting one another, loving one another, living in harmony with one another, waiting for one another before eating, and, most dramatically, "through love becom[ing] slaves to one another" (Gal. 5:13). To be perichoretically related to one another through Christ is not merely to *interact* but to live in *interdependence,* to "rejoice with those who rejoice, weep with those who weep" (Rom. 12:15). Again, the "togetherness of Christians is . . . not secondary or contingent: it is integral to their life *just as is their abiding in Christ*."[10]

As we do so, we demonstrate a quality of living that the world is yearning for and through which humans have been created to thrive.[11] In the Bible, bonding is far more important than blood. We see this especially in marriage. "Therefore a man leaves his father and mother," whom he is related to by blood, "and clings to his wife, and they become one flesh" (Gen. 2:24). As a young adult, getting married, I enjoyed the notion of bonding over blood. It felt romantic and exciting to think of my new bride and me as closer than kin. But now as a parent to two children, I can't believe it. I can hardly fathom that my children will someday bond with someone more than with me and their mother. But, in the Bible, the new marriage relationship is now the priority over blood. Even more, Jesus tells us that our commitment to him supersedes our families (Luke 14:26) and that we will be more bonded to Christians than we are to unbelieving relatives (Mark 3:33–35).

My sister Carrie is one of the dearest people in my life. I am deeply bonded to her, but we share absolutely no blood, because she is my adopted stepsister. When people see us together they naturally assume that we are blood-related because of how close we are to each other and how attached she is to my wife and kids. Though we are not blood-related, my bonding with my sister means that we are much closer than I am to a number of cousins and aunts and uncles to whom I am blood-related.

The experience I have had with my sister is also the experience I have had with a number of Christian friends. The faith we share is the only truly enduring reality. This is why as a parent, I cannot count on blood but need to develop deep Christian bonding with my children. As a parent I rejoice in the faith of my children so that as they grow they will not just be my children but will also become my brother and sister in Christ.

While the divine Persons are by nature a communion, human persons require covenantal commitment in order to effect the kind of perichoretic interdependence necessary for transformation.[12] Therefore, Christian communities are formed intentionally through expressed Christian faith and commitment to the community.

For our church, this means we take very seriously both our baptismal vows offered as a community and the responsibility to lead people to a personal faith in Christ. In agreement with our church's constitution, we ensure that all church members be confessing Christians, committed to being formed by the Holy Spirit as part of the body of Christ.[13] Faith in Christ and a commitment to relationships within the body of Christ are inextricable. Further, Christian baptism, whether of infants or adults, requires a commitment not only to Christ but to "participate responsibly in the worship and mission of the church." This baptismal confession of faith is always met with the response of the congregation to pray for and support the baptized in the Christian faith.

It is hard to overstate the importance of the communal exchange taking place in this sacramental moment. Miroslav Volf cites Matthew 18:20 ("For where two or three are gathered in my name, I am there among them") to assert that "Christ's presence is promised not to the believing individual directly, but rather to the entire congregation, and only through the latter to the individual. *This is why no one can come to faith alone and live in faith alone.*"[14]

The early church understood and taught that to be baptized as a Christian meant to undergo an "extraordinary thoroughgoing resocialization" so that the community of believers "would become virtually the primary group for its members supplanting all other loyalties."[15] Through this relational restructuring of the Spirit, the believer progresses in depth of faith (relationship to God) and in transformation into the likeness of God (understood in relational terms and expressed in relationships with other believers—see 2 Cor. 3:17–18; John 13:14–15). Indeed, as the "fruit of the Spirit" (Gal. 5:22–26) attests, relational maturity is virtually indistinguishable from spiritual maturity, and the spirituality of a community is defined by the quality of the relationships formed.[16]

When I was a relatively young Christian, my family was in a time of turmoil. My parents had gone through a divorce, and we stopped going to church. As a college student and a staff member for Youth for Christ, I was asked to serve on the evangelism committee of my church. And at my first meeting I met Howard and Alice Thomas, a dear elderly couple. At the end of the night we prayed together, and they mentioned a dozen people or more. They prayed with a sense of passion and care for these people, none of whom were their own children. Afterward I went up to them and told them, "I'm so deeply touched by the way you pray for these people. It's like the way I picture parents praying for their children." I had never met Howard and Alice Thomas before that night. But Howard looked at me and said, "We will pray for you every day. What is your name, son?" They put my picture on their refrigerator. When I got married, Beth's picture was added and when my children came along, theirs too. Until first Howard and then Alice died, they prayed for me every day. Today, in no small part because of those prayers, all of the members of my family confess Christ and my mother and stepfather are both elders in the Presbyterian church. That is the kind of relationship that we have to offer the world—prayerful interdependence lived out because of Christ by the Spirit.

At a funeral for a housemate, a young man who lives in what used to be called an "orphanage" stood up to speak. In halting words he talked about his friend who had become like a brother to him. As he held back tears he said, "I have heard that blood is thicker than water. But love is thicker than both."

Sacramental: The Presence of God Revealed in the Ordinary

> The term "sacrament" . . . embraces generally all those signs which God has ever enjoined upon men to render them more certain and confident of the truth of his promises.[17]

> Sacraments "offer unto our sight those things which inwardly (God) performs for us, and so strengthens our hearts and increases our faith through the working of God's Spirit in our hearts."[18]

If the perichoretic, relational dynamic of "Living the Trinity" is the inner experience of Christian life, then the "sacramental" dynamic is the way that the Christian community lives within and reveals the presence of God in everyday life. For Calvin, because God made the world and because all of creation lends itself to divine use, God can employ any of it sacramentally to us.[19]

In the same way that the Spirit brings union with Christ in the sacrament as a "gracious personal presence" and brings the believer into union by faith, that same relational-sacramental Spirit brings, in the everyday world apart from the celebrating of sacramental events, similar revelation of God's presence.[20] Because God has blessed matter by using it as sacramental elements, all material things, all the elements of this world are able to be used to enhance the revelation of God's presence.[21] While the celebration of the sacraments themselves serves as a reminder to us that we are dependent upon both the spiritual and the material, to live sacramentally is to live within the everyday life connected to God's living Word. In short, *communal life is sacramental life,* and God uses ordinary elements to reveal his extraordinary presence.[22]

One of the great joys of being a pastor is being part of the ordinary but holy moments of everyday life. I have been with nervous brides and grooms as they choked back tears and said their wedding vows, and I have stood with couples who recommitted in love to each other after fifty years of marriage. I have held babies for baptism and cradled the body of an elder in my church as he passed on to glory. I have had meals that didn't include just good food and wine, but also prayers, laughter, and tears. I have watched a three-year-old boy walk with his teddy bear into brain surgery, and I have turned away as a man wept tears of joy for the healing of his wife.

If a sacrament is the "mystery" of God's presence in common elements, then the truest sacrament is, as Wolfhart Pannenberg has said, nothing less than the frail, faulty, and fickle people of God who in every circumstance reveal the Spirit of God present with us.[23] Since the ordinary people of God are the truest "sacrament" on earth, it shouldn't stun me so that the central ritual of the Christian life is the most ordinary experience in human life: eating. The enduring tradition of Christian life is to gather around a dinner table.

What Jesus gave us when he left his disciples was a meal to remember him by and to proclaim his ministry until he personally returns. The way we celebrate that meal and live out the implications of it serve as a mysterious sign of God's life-transforming communion available through the church to all people.[24]

A Word about WORD and . . . Sacrament.

At my ordination as a "Minister of Word and Sacrament," my friend Mark Roberts reminded the congregation that we are far more a church of WORD and sacrament.

Indeed, in the evangelical tradition, we are a people of the book. I too heartily affirm and honor the ministry of Word. However, historically, the preaching of the word has been the primary practice of the Christian tradition, and the sacraments have been relegated to a place of lesser importance. Calvin helps us restore that balance by describing the church as the community where the stories that define the community as Christian are told and the sacraments are displayed, confirming and demonstrating the realities of those stories to us in the here and now.[25] As a senior pastor, I am privileged to preach most every week, and I believe that preaching is crucial to the spirituality of the church, when it is rightly understood as a *communal* activity of the people of God, rather than as a solitary experience of hearing a message. But a relational-sacramental spirituality will necessarily restore the sacraments to a more prominent place in the practices of the church for the following reasons.

First and foremost, it cannot be emphasized strongly enough that for Calvin, the sacraments are the primary way in which the real presence of the risen Christ establishes, maintains, nourishes, and empowers, through the Holy Spirit, a transforming union with the believer. "Nothing short of true and full communion with the crucified and risen Christ is what is at stake . . . in the sacrament."[26]

Second, sacraments are themselves *relational events* given to us by God to help us overcome our "mistrust" of God. They are "methods employed by the graciousness of God to express and develop a gracious *personal relationship* with him."[27]

Third, the Lord's Supper especially demonstrates the necessity of Christian fellowship and Christian witness.[28] An analysis of 1 Corinthians 11:27–34 reveals that Paul's critique of the Corinthians' "unworthy eating" is entirely social. "Paul was not concerned with the intrinsic moral condition of the individuals . . . but rather with the lack of appreciation for the communal implications of the celebration of the Eucharist."[29] Wealthier members of the congregation would arrive early and be finished (and sated!) with the meal before the other members arrived. What was intended to be a celebration of a community sharing and participating in the life of Christ was instead just another supper clique that reflected the divisions of Corinthian society. As Paul had written earlier in the letter, "the cup of blessing that we bless, is it not a sharing in the blood of Christ? The bread that we break, is it not a sharing in the body of Christ? Because there is one bread, we who are many are one body, for we all partake of the one bread" (1 Cor. 10:16–17). As I often remind my congregation, the celebration of the Lord's Supper requires other Christians (even for pastors). You can pray alone, study alone, sing alone, or serve alone, but you cannot celebrate sacraments by yourself.

Further, for Paul, the Lord's Supper was not strictly speaking a "religious" event. It was an everyday and public event that through eating and drinking "proclaimed" the Lord's death and the salvation through it.[30] In other words, the central activity of the Christian tradition given by the Lord as a fitting remembrance of his life and sacrificial death is in itself a relational event meant to reveal, in the everyday world, the saving presence of Christ. Even more, this encounter happens among ordinary people through very common elements. Scripture urges us to view the Lord's Supper as the most ordinary of events. In 1 Corinthians 11 what is depicted is much more a family meal, with the usual "dysfunction," than a religious ceremony conducted to the harmonies of Bach, played on an organ, accompanied by a choir, and utilizing silver serving pieces.

The human elements of bread and wine, hands and mouths, gathered together, breaking and pouring, blessing and giving, eating and drinking are from the most common human experience, meals. Jesus seemed to break all customs about eating, spurning formality and fussiness, caring little about the character of those who ate with him.[31] For him, it was an act of friendship and basic necessity, a most ordinary experience where people came to expect the extraordinary because of his presence and where consequently people were saved and transformed.

The story of Zacchaeus in Luke 19 is the quintessential example of a person whose life was transformed simply by the invitation from and eating of dinner with Jesus. No sermon was recorded, no miracle took place: just the salvation of God brought to a man through shared bread and drink—a relationship with Jesus in everyday circumstances transforming a human life.

The Lord's Supper is both a demonstration of the promises of God and an invitation to enter into the promises through Christ's community constituted by the Holy Spirit. Ministers are not the real celebrants of the sacraments, but the whole church is the royal priesthood. Whether we gather in homes, come to the front of the congregation to receive the elements, or sit in pews, we are gathered as one family around a common "table," as it were, passing the elements hand to hand, blessing one another, and sharing the bread-and-cup fellowship of the Eternal Table hosted through the Spirit by the incarnate Christ.

Relational-Sacramental Spirituality

Relational-sacramental spirituality, then, describes the Triune Life at work. Since the being of God is communion and the expression of that communion is expressed in everyday life, then all spirituality that leads to transformation according to the likeness of the Triune God will necessarily be both relational (in and expressing of communion) and sacramental (through the means of everyday life). This spirituality is not a privatized or other-worldly spirituality but, reflecting the Trinity, is a spirituality that from start to finish is experienced within communion and into the world in perichoretic interdependence of Christians upon each other by God's Spirit. By recovering a spiritual theology of the Trinity, we will recover a relational-sacramental spirituality that *begins in community and transforms the disciple of Christ through a living communion with Christ, serving as witness to the activity of the Triune God in the world.*

G. C. Berkouwer warns that the emphasis upon affirming communion with Christ in the Lord's Supper often leads to a view of the Lord's Supper as an interruption of the "desert life" with the "oasis of communion." Instead, he wrote, there is actually continuity between the sacrament and "normal life":

> We do not see the Lord's Supper as an interruption (of everyday life) which stands without relations as a strange mystical rapture, *but as a communion exercise in the light of the act and institution of Christ which is oriented toward the fullness of everyday life.*[32]

Once we realize that the icon of God as a heavenly table fellowship depicts an eternal reality of God's own character and nature, then we realize that we are indeed called to be people of the table. It is also as the people at that table that we have something utterly life- and world-transforming to offer to seekers. As we live in perichoretic interdependence with one another, we offer a glimpse of God's own life present to us.

In the movie *Places in the Heart,* Sally Field plays a proud, fiercely independent woman in the South, whose husband is accidentally killed by a drunken young black man. It was an accident, but in that southern town in the middle of the last century, the boy is immediately lynched and dragged through the town.

For the rest of the movie, Sally Field has to struggle to save the family farm. She resists help and spurns all charity. She is determined and capable, but the task is too enormous for her. She takes in a blind boarder to make ends meet, but that isn't enough. Just as she is at wit's end, help comes in the form of another African-American man, a vagabond played by Danny Glover. Finally, Field must accept Glover's help as well as the assistance of her blind boarder. After considerable toil and struggle the farm is saved. But as the story ends, you sense that more has happened here than meets the eye. This is not just the story of economic survival, but of lives that are transformed through their interdependence upon each other. A disabled boarder becomes a valuable contributor, a wanderer finds friendship and dignity, and a proud, independent woman finds both healing for her grieving heart and a perspective of redemption that is bigger than any one harvest. At the end of the movie, Field, Glover, and the blind boarder all give thanks for the harvest by going to church. As they sing "Blessed Assurance" they take Communion, passing the Communion plate one to another.

The blind man passes the Communion plate to Danny Glover, whispering the words "the body of Christ." He then passes it to Sally Field, saying, "the body of Christ," and then—unexpectedly—she passes it to her (dead) husband, who then passes the tray to the (also dead) young man who killed him. And in that moment you have a glimpse of eternity. At that Communion table in that small church in that dusty town so caught up in the ordinary struggles of harvest life and southern segregation, even those who are separated by life and death are together; even those who cause sin against one another or harm to one another are unified. In that moment the kingdom is revealed. It's beautiful; it's breathtaking. And it's a momentary vision of what Christian faith and church life should be, in the words of G. C. Berkouwer, in the "fullness of everyday life."

As Lloyd-Jones's charge says, we must be producing an exceptional order of living. But alas, so many of our churches that celebrate the ritual do not see the life-altering results. In the next section, I take up the central *practices* of the faith, namely, worship, word, and witness. Through reconnecting them to this understanding of trinitarian communion, I will demonstrate how those practices are to be performed in a life-transforming way.

PART 3

An Exceptional Community: Life-Transforming Practices

6

Transforming Worship I

Performing for God

"The church of Christ is summoned into being by God in order to be a *worshipping community.*"[1]

Ralph Martin

Last year, I was watching an episode of one my favorite television shows, *The West Wing,* in which cellist Yo-Yo Ma played a private concert at the White House. I thought to myself, Now, that has to be one of the best parts of being president. Right up there with having your own jet and knowing for certain whether there are UFOs in Area 51, one of the very best parts about being president is that if you want to have Yo-Yo Ma come to your house and play the cello, he will. In fact, if you are president you can get any performer you want because it's your birthday or just because it's Wednesday. Do you want Tony Bennett to sing a few songs? Done. Do you want Eric Clapton to come play some blues guitar? No problem. Do you want Diana Krall to play piano? Sure. Because you are the president, and your wish is a command. These performers *have* to come. It is called a "command performance."

The tradition goes back to the days of the monarchy commanding special performances of plays and concertos and the like. Certainly, some other people would fill in the audience, and the monarch used the performance to say something to the masses about his or her benevolence, but the performance was *for* the king or queen. And while we don't have "official" command performances today, the tradition still exists. Thus, if the president asks a performer to come, he or she is likely to come.

So, let me ask you a question, if you were president and wanted to have someone do a command performance, who would you have? Now let me ask you a different question. *If God were holding a command performance, who do you think he'd have?* If God could have anybody come and perform for him, who do you think he'd summon? The answer to this one is in the Bible. The answer is YOU. You, and me, and all of God's people. And that is exactly what happens every Sunday. God calls for a command performance, and we are requested to do our thing. In God's eyes, you are Yo-Yo Ma. You are called upon and commanded to perform. Yes, there may be others there watching you and your people, and God is using the performance to communicate something of his benevolence and goodness to all his "subjects," but the performance is for him.

That is what worship is all about. It is a display, a performance, commanded by God so that all of creation may see the life-transforming glory of God through his people. *Our worship is a command performance for God and the world that transforms our lives.*

Worship and the Exceptional Life

I have been attempting to demonstrate that the "exceptional life" is the very life the Triune God enacted and made visible through the communal life of the people of God. In this and the following chapter, we will see that the worship of God is an essential part of the display. How we worship demonstrates to all of humanity the purpose for their very existence, and by our transformed lives we offer a response to the challenges of "spiritual seekers" who are increasingly rejecting Christian churches in their search for a satisfying spirituality.

However, it should be noted from the outset that the *primary* purpose of worship is *not* to "meet the challenge of the world" nor even in the first instance to transform people.[2] Worship is not just a warm-up act for teaching or preaching, nor is it primarily about inspiring people at all.[3] Worship is fundamentally about praising and honoring God, revealing God's grace and love. In short, *glorifying* God.[4]

Charles Hodge gives a classic description demonstrating that even our salvation is ultimately for inspiring worship: "The purpose of redemption, therefore, is to *exhibit* the grace of God in such a conspicuous manner as to fill all hearts with wonder and all lips with praise."[5] Worship gives to God what God alone is due: the praise of his glory (Isa. 43:11; Eph. 1:12,14).

This glory is not revealed so much in great solos or spellbinding preaching *as through the transformed lives of people who encounter the living God in worship*. Geoffrey Wainright has written, "Believers may render God glory by a kind of reflection, as they are changed into his likeness, 'from glory to glory.' They glorify God as they grow in conformity with his character."[6] So the performance, as it were, is both for God and a means of making the performers *like* God.True worship flows from the nature of the Triune God.[7] When we understand this, then we see that regardless of the size of church or the worship style, if our goal is to reveal God to people in a life-transforming way, then it is exactly a "performance"—an *enactment* of the ministry of the Triune God by the people of God.

The Command Performance

Enactment means, literally, "theatrical representation" or "performance." While it is often said that our worship should not be a "performance," in the sense of just being a theatrical "show," it must be a performance in a more profound sense. As such, it is intended to be "acted out" on a universal stage for the sake of God's glory, initiated by God as scriptwriter (and audience!), led by Jesus Christ, accompanied by and for the transformation of the participants, witnessing to the world as a setting for the Divine Play. At the heart of this "enactment of trinitarian grace"[8] is the celebration and rehearsing of God's saving deeds or, to use Robert Webber's phrase, "the Gospel in motion."[9] It is an event recalling an event that has the power to transform human lives.

As performance, trinitarian worship must always have three simultaneous orientations. First, worship is *theological* enactment of the reality of God discovered as Trinity in the encounter with the saving Jesus. It is not, fundamentally, the creative action of humanity, but participation in *God's* action[10] that displays the communion of the Son with the Father by the Holy Spirit in the loving and saving mission to the world. Therefore, the performance must be according to the Divine Scriptwriter and Director.

Second, worship is also the enactment of *historical* events. It does not celebrate the past but "proclaims the meaning of the original event and confronts worshippers with the claim of God on their lives"[11] in the present. Worship is according to the biblical "script" and connects believers with a real history that gives present-tense "direction" by the Spirit. As such, tradition can neither be spurned nor be glorified. The salvation-history of the people of God must be recalled and given contemporary expression.

Third, worship is a *communal* enactment of God's presence. It actually accomplishes a meeting between God and his people. The enacted communion is experienced and deepened through worship as a kind of holy participation in Christ (1 Cor. 10:26).

By maintaining these three orientations, our worship becomes, as Robert Webber describes, an expression and a deepening of our communion with the Triune God. In worship we are invited to join to be embraced in the divine communion. We respond by offering ourselves to God and become a participant in God's community through this life-transforming performance.

> In baptism, preaching and the Eucharist we act out a story. The story has to do with what God has done for us and our response to God's work. It is an enactment of the event that gives meaning and purpose to our life.[12]

Worship, as the visible enactment of God's trinitarian grace, has three movements with three crucial parts to play.[13] First, it is an enactment by the Triune God with God as the scriptwriter and director. Second, it is an enactment with and for the Triune God with Christ as the leader, the church as the performers and God as the audience. And finally, it is an act that consequently brings about a transformation for worshipers through the presence of God as a display to the world.

God as Scriptwriter and Director

According to the Reformers, only God initiates worship.[14] As Philip Butin has demonstrated, for Calvin, "the trinitarian activity of worship began with the 'downward' movement of the Father's revelation of divine grace through the Son, by the means of the Holy Spirit."[15] If the first movement of worship is the trinitarian expression of God himself, then our worship practices must always be judged by how well they reflect God's direction and example. The primary questions are not about relevance to the world, or inspiration for people, *but faithfulness and submission to God.* This begins in the necessary and honest affirmation that *we gather to worship God at God's gracious invitation and that the gathering merits us nothing*. Even in our gathering we are responding to the "command performance" of a sovereign Lord who honors us by inviting us into his presence. This is in itself grace—grace that when accepted leads to participation, which is the second movement of the Transforming Performance.

Christ as Leader of a Church of Performers

Now imagine, if you will, that Yo-Yo Ma received an invitation from the president and responded only one out of every four times. The president calls for a performance, but he says, "Nah, it's my only day to sleep in." Or "I really want to work in the garden." Or "The beach is looking great today." Or what if he thought that the purpose of the evening wasn't for him to perform, but to be part of the audience, and so he came unprepared? What if Yo-Yo forgot his cello? Or what if every time he was on way home from the White House, he turned to his wife and said, "You know, I didn't get much out of that." What would you do if you heard about this? You'd say to him, "Look, I know that you are a big important star, but this is the president of the United States. You have been asked—no, commanded—to perform. It is your duty. You are the performer. He is the audience. The point is *not* whether you get anything out of it!"

But this is exactly the trap we can fall into when thinking about worship. Unfortunately, many Christians who know that they're saved and know that their salvation isn't based on works can find it too easy to believe that the invitation to perform is really no big deal. They can sneak in quietly and sit in the back whenever they want—maybe once a month or so if there are no sporting events or it's not a particularly beautiful day. They believe that they really aren't expected to *do* anything. And they believe that if they come, then the result should be that *they* are entertained, or moved, or inspired.

Perhaps the most important thing to understand when you come to worship is that you are on stage. Most of us come into worship either wiping the sleep out of our eyes or concerned about finding a good seat. What we should be doing is clearing our throats, warming up our voices, and preparing our hearts. Throughout the Psalms we hear one call to worship after another. They vary in their wording, but they all say the same thing: "Worshipers! Showtime!" Psalm 66: 1–2 puts it this way: *"Make a joyful noise to God, all the earth; sing the glory of his name."*

Now, some of us are going to be uncomfortable with all this talk about performance. We say, "Worship shouldn't be a performance; it should be sincere." As if they were incompatible. Or when we hear the word *performance,* we think that it then requires a high level of ability. We demur, "Oh, I can't sing. I don't pray aloud very well. I certainly can't preach. I'll just sit here, while the professionals perform."

Notice again that the psalm says to make a joyful *noise* to the Lord. It seems to imply that as long as the noise is truly full of joy, a true expression of our sincere feelings, it doesn't much matter if we are all that good at it.

I was reminded of this when I sat through my son's third-grade end-of-the-year patriotic show—a bunch of eight- and nine-year-olds singing "America the Beautiful," "This Land Is Your Land," and "The Star-Spangled Banner." It was (how shall I put this?) *enthusiastic*. It was sincere, sweet, and somewhat on-key. Was it a performance? Certainly. Did that make it any less sincere an expression of our children's love for their country? Certainly not. It wasn't "Up with People," and it certainly wasn't something you'd put on TV, but do you think even one of those appointment-skipping, video-camera-toting, crammed-in-like-sardines parents cared one little bit? Of course not. Because we love those little Yankee Doodle dandies, and they genuinely did their best.

And perhaps that is the best metaphor for us. We are giving a command performance for the One who is our Father, who loves and only wants us to sincerely and enthusiastically give our best. Over and over again, the Psalms tell us "Sing *to* the Lord." We are the performers for God. That is what makes this more than just a human expression of talents and abilities. God is the audience we wish to please.

The Other Audience

If you turn on Christian television you'll often hear people say that they gather to worship God to "receive a blessing"—like the purpose of coming to worship is what God does for us. Of course, they are missing the whole point. God is the audience and we perform for him. The blessing of worship for us is *blessing God*. It is being in God's presence and enjoying fellowship with God. Nichols calls us back to the model of the early Reformers when he writes that "we must recognize that they went to worship not to do something for God, nor even to get something from God, but far more *to be something with God*."[16] With the result that God would be glorified, revealed, honored, and revered, and not just among us, but throughout *all the earth*. Our worship is for God as our audience, but it is for the world's benefit.

Psalm 66:1–3 says, *Make a joyful noise to God, all the earth; sing the glory of his name; give to him glorious praise*. God calls us to give a command performance that will reveal his presence, that will shed light upon him; that will give him glory *in all the earth*. We are to give worship to God worthy of his greatness, a performance that will reveal his goodness and his grace to others—especially those who do not know him or worship him. And the result, according to Psalm 66:5, is a call to all the world: *Come and see what God has done: he is awesome in his deeds among mortals.*

Command performances were not just offered by kings for their own pleasure, but as gifts to the people as a way of demonstrating the king's kindness and care. A good performance reflected well on the king who commanded it. And that is what we are to do. Our worship is for God as the audience but for the world's benefit.

The final word about trinitarian worship is that we who have been invited into communion with God need to give our whole selves to God in response. It is far more about our intentional wholehearted participation than anything else. And learning that is what the next chapter is all about.

7

Transforming Worship II

Worship That Changes Things

Being a pastor in a beach town does have its drawbacks. If the sun is shining and a warm, well-shaped swell is coming in, the attendance tends to drop a bit. The beauty of the ocean, the heat of the sun, a chance to a have few unhurried moments playing in the sand with your kids . . . I hear the same thoughts from so many people that I am not even surprised anymore: "I just worship God better on the beach with my family than in a pew with church people."

I appreciate and understand their sentiments. I too enjoy nature and love to be with my family. Sometimes those moments are so acutely blessed that I am awed and moved to tears. But that is not worship.

Worship is not what you feel when you look at the ocean or when you are enjoying a wonderful mountain lake. It's not the way you feel smelling the cut grass of a perfectly manicured golf course or hearing the squeak of perfect dry snow under your skis. Many of us confuse worship with inspiration. Inspiration occurs when God illumines our lives with his gracious presence. Worship is our response to those moments. If we truly want to honor the God who gave us perfect swells, clear trout streams, ski slopes, golf greens, beautiful children, and loving spouses, we should enjoy those things six days a week and then give God the worship he commands on the seventh. Worship *always* includes gathering with God's people and participating in "spirit and in truth" (John 4:24). Biblically speaking there is no such thing as passive worship or individual worship. All worship is participatory and corporate. That leads us to some specific transforming worship practices.

Worship Begins in the Streets

Throughout the Bible, God calls all of creation to worship him by gracious invitation and with specific instructions,[1] including telling people that "God is the host of public worship," welcoming his people in hospitality, and enabling worship through his gracious self-giving. Indeed, God is the "prompter,"[2] inspiring the congregation to give themselves to God and outsiders in response to the invitation.[3]

Surprisingly, the first aspect of worship therefore is not the introit, invocation, or even prayers of thanksgiving, but the gathering of people for worship. Inspired by God's own ministry of initiating communion with people, the church that performs for God and the world begins the worship service in the streets, towns, and homes by inviting people to worship. Evangelism is therefore the beginning of worship. It is telling people the good news that God is personally inviting every person to come before him and become part of his people.[4]

As Patrick Keifert demonstrates, the Israelites' awareness that they were welcomed by God led to an obligation that they welcome the stranger into their midst.[5] Biblically, worship is always a "public" event where all are invited and shown hospitality, [6] and the contemporary tendency to assert that worship is for believers and not for "seekers" is a contradiction of both God's word and God's character as seen in the Trinity.[7] Contrary to what was long-accepted popular wisdom, most first contacts with churches by the unchurched now come through unannounced visitors anonymously "checking out" a church in their worship service.[8]

For many churches, however, worship is reduced to "family time," playing out what Keifert has referred to as the "ideology of intimacy," where activities that are meant to be public are instead translated into and valued for their privatized experiences. These churches actually are hindered in their ministry of hospitality and evangelism to outsiders, because the ideology of intimacy inevitably excludes the very people whom they wish to include. They speak of being a "warm and real community," yet there are often no agreed-upon public rituals, avenues, or hosts for a stranger or outsider to find his or her way into the shared corporate life of the fellowship.

While not intending to criticize smaller churches (indeed larger churches can function the same way), Keifert warns single-cell churches (those of fewer than 250 people in worship) that they "tend to devalue the public nature of the liturgy and turn it into the worship of the extended family. Both liturgy as public worship and evangelism as public witness to the Gospel suffer in private pastoral-theological strategies."[9] He suggests that worship that demonstrates hospitality and is effective in evangelism is a matter of churches "opening [their] private world to a public one, of gaining competence to participate in the customs of public life, of learning to enjoy life among strangers."[10] This public dimension is the link to worship as an enactment that is intentionally "performed" in the wider arena of the world.

Show Up and Get with It!

It is worth remembering that over and over again, the primary instruction of worship is to "come." Come and see what God has done. Come and worship. Come and enter his temple. Come together as God's people. Remember that all of the calls to worship in the Psalms were public and corporate calls. They were personal calls, yes, but not individual calls. Which leads to this very important and often overlooked point: To worship God correctly, you must come to church. Worship is a command performance where God invites you into his house and asks you to join in worship with all of his people, giving voice for and witnessing to all of creation.

At the very least, anchoring worship in the Trinity reminds us that there is both a corporate necessity and an individual responsibility to continue meeting together (Heb. 10:25), something that becomes more and more relevant with each passing year. As I discussed earlier, recent studies have documented that the increase in committed believers over the past two decades has not resulted in increased worship attendance or church membership.[11]

While I am grateful for the proliferation of worship music and sermon tapes that bring various elements of worship to individuals in the "privacy" of their own home and car, I do believe that they can lead inadvertently to less genuine worship participation. As "connoisseurs" (and paying customers!) of worship music, it is tempting to judge worship-leading as we would any other product or performance. These resources usually feature the finest quality of "production," only increasing the temptation to pass on the local gathering, where there is not the same degree of excellence. I am not criticizing these materials—quite the opposite. The availability of worship tapes and sermons has certainly strengthened individual believers and encouraged some positive trends in worship. However, passively listening to music and sermon tapes does not equal "participating" in the trinitarian enactment of worship.[12]

Further, when the church does gather, the "royal priesthood" often relinquishes its corporate and active participation and instead allows pastors, musicians, and other designated worship leaders to be the proxy worshipers. This tendency to be spectators rather than participants is common in any style of worship. Whether it is the high cathedral church whose choir and paid soloists do most of the singing, a Bible teaching church that views worship participation as taking lengthy notes, a seeker service of "presentation evangelism," or a liturgical church where the participation is rote and perfunctory, the lack of full heart-felt engagement keeps the church from worshiping in "spirit" if not in "truth."

Obviously, it doesn't have to be this way. Mutual ministry in a 1 Corinthians 14 model can be the expectation, where friends and family are encouraged to minister to one another and the whole congregation offers prayers and exhortations. Choral pieces and soloists can become "cantors" leading the congregation in a call and response, or part of the "proclamation" as a sung sermon. Sermons can lead directly into responsive acts inspiring and guiding the congregation as they fully participate in praise, commitment, and the sacraments, or in mutually edifying ministry. Life events in the community of faith can be commemorated and connected to the biblical tradition by the writing of worship songs where we together express our praise to God. Sacraments can be celebrated in more communal ways, where each person sees himself or herself as offering a word of institution as we share communion or a prayer of blessing upon the newly baptized.

For paid clergy and worship leaders, worship as trinitarian participation means their contribution is measured by the extent to which worshipers are equipped to become participants.[13] If pastors and worship leaders take this role seriously, then the church will continuously reevaluate the accessibility and theological veracity of worship. Following the Reformers' model, a contemporary plan of "education and adaptation" would be a regular feature of worship life. While adaptation can and does lead naturally to contemporizing worship, education reminds us that the meaning and significance of some of the most basic elements of the service of worship (Lord's Supper, doxology, "passing of the peace," Lord's Prayer, giving, etc.) will need to be continually taught.[14]

More Sacraments, with More Leaders

Trinitarian participation also raises the question of the biblical rationale for limiting the leadership of sacramental acts to ordained clergy. It seems far more consistent with the New Testament sense of the "priesthood of all believers" (based on passages like 1 Peter 2:9–11) to have the sacraments "approved" and "ordered" by the congregation as a whole (with whatever leadership structures are used), and the words of institution "celebrated" by virtually anyone in the congregation who has been duly instructed by the pastors. Indeed, pastors are necessary for the church to be faithful in rightful practicing of the sacraments, but their main function should be to equip and inform (Eph. 4:1–12) and not act in a "priestly" way. Indeed, in this regard, the Reformed ordination of clergy to the ministry of Word and sacrament seems out of step with the conviction of the priesthood of all believers and the pastors' central biblical responsibility to "equip the saints" for ministry.

Larger churches would do well to consider how, through home fellowship and small groups, the celebration of the whole community could then be continued in a more intimate environment where everyone could be more fully involved in praying, caring for one another, mutual admonition, and sharing the Lord's Supper.[15] A sense that Christ is the leader of worship could enable a congregation to begin worship of God in the sanctuary gathered together and then progress to places where the church "scattered" could take up the worship of God in different locales. Shared liturgy, trained lay leaders, and common texts could be offered so that all may participate in one service of worship, albeit in different and more convivial settings.

Communal Preaching

Traditionally and rightly, the sermon is an act of worship. It is the fruit of prayer, a work of God's Spirit in the body of Christ; it is the doxological witness to the grace of God in Christ. It is set in the praise and prayer of the worshiping congregation. It calls Christians to communion with God and sends them out into a life of Christian service.[16] But the conviction that worship demands congregational participation might at first glance seem contradictory to the customary emphasis on preaching,[17] and some of the proponents of worship renewal have begun to question the centrality of preaching as an act of worship.[18]

I contend that preaching is indispensable to worship and crucial to the spirituality of the church, but that for it to be performed rightly and in a biblically transforming manner requires two emphases:

1. Preaching must be understood as an act of the community.
2. Preaching must be linked more intentionally to the sacraments.

When the Word is preached, God is present—when preaching is unalterably connected to the *gathered assembly for worship.*[19] By "joining his Spirit" with the Word of Christ, God himself ensures its efficacy and "inspires" faith.[20] This was so important to the Reformers that Calvin criticized those who, bored with less-than-gifted teachers, eschewed gatherings to study on their own.

It is also important to remember that the Reformers' situation was, in many ways, the opposite of our own. The Reformation proclaimed the liberty and responsibility of the individual over and against the collectivism and mechanism of the medieval Catholic Church. The preached word replaced the Mass as a new sacrifice, and personal trust in God through Christ became the channel of God's gracious intervention in a person's life.

Yet today, it is individualism, not collectivism, that is prevalent in the church and culture. The spiritual seekers of the world are looking for union with God (or some other equivalent) in a day in which even Christians believe that being tied to the church formally is not "necessary for faith," viewing churches "less as sources of faith than as resources for their personal, family religious, or spiritual needs."[21] Furthermore, as a recent study has demonstrated, even with all the proliferation of media-based biblical content available, American Christians know less about their beliefs and live them out more superficially and less consistently than ever before.[22] Could it be that the Protestant pulpit and all of the "practical messages" so preferred by baby boomers are not increasing communion, helping people connect with God, give themselves in worship, or grow spiritually as much as we think?

In a day when biblical content is available virtually every minute via radio, television, cassette tapes, books, and computer programs, it is important to hold firm the Reformed conviction of the special, distinct nature of the preaching *event,* which takes place within the community of faith.

> The Preaching of the word of God is the Word of God. Wherefore, when this Word of God is now preached in the church by ministers lawfully called, we believe that the very Word of God is proclaimed, and received by the faithful.[23]

Preaching is not merely an instrument of education or therapy but instead a transformative spiritual encounter of God's own presence speaking to us (individually and corporately) and calling us to respond. Further, the telling and retelling of the biblical narratives, so important in spiritual formation (as we will discuss in the next chapter), takes place in all of the worship service and not in the sermon alone. The whole service, including the use of creeds, prayers, and eucharistic words of institution, is meant to be a retelling of salvation history and a continual contemporary response to that story.[24]

Preaching, then, must be primarily an expression of the presence of the Triune God with and for the community, an activity of the whole people of God that fosters communion, rather than a solitary experience of hearing a "message for living." It must call the gathered church to faithful participation as the trinitarian Communion of God by proclaiming the saving reality of God, grounding them in their shared narratives, instructing in obedience, and "sacramentally" revealing God. Ultimately, worship is not just the warm-up for the preaching; instead, preaching must foster *worship* that "lifts us up out of ourselves to participate in the very life and communion of the Godhead, that life and communion for which we were created."[25]

Additionally, my seminary preaching professor, the late Dr. Ian Pitt-Watson used to remind his students that "we don't preach *to* the congregation, we preach *for* them." The preacher is not some disconnected divine mouthpiece but is also a recipient of the very Word that he or she is proclaiming. In this way, preaching is always "local talk" about divine things. As one who preaches every week, I am aware that my preparation includes not only good exegesis, prayerful reflection, and finding good stories for application, but also listening to what the Spirit is doing in my congregation. My job is to reveal to the community what God is saying to and doing in the community, and most of the time what God is saying or doing in me, as the preacher, is only one very small part.

So in our church in San Clemente we believe that worship begins in the streets and ends in small groups. It begins (as we have said) in reaching out to others with the welcome of God who invites us to worshipful communion. It reaches a climax in the service of Word and sacrament. But it is completed in small groups that meet in homes on Sunday evening to eat a meal together, review the sermon, study a bit deeper, and support each other as we live out the call of God in the sermon. It is from start to finish a communal event that requires a personal response.

Once we restore preaching to its proper focus as a communal event creating an encounter between God and his people, then we are ready

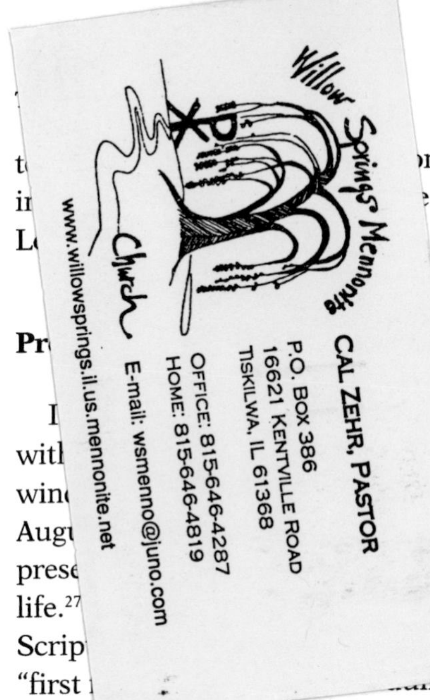

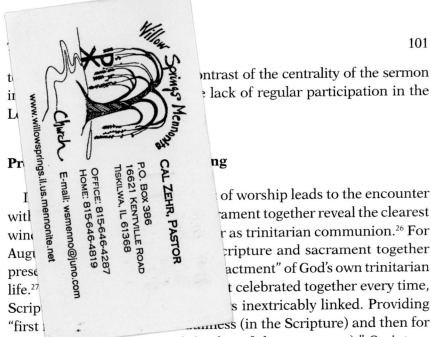

t[illegible] ontrast of the centrality of the sermon i[illegible] lack of regular participation in the L[illegible]

Pr[illegible]ng

I[illegible] of worship leads to the encounter wit[illegible]ament together reveal the clearest win[illegible]r as trinitarian communion.[26] For Aug[illegible]cripture and sacrament together pres[illegible]actment" of God's own trinitarian life.[27] [illegible]t celebrated together every time, Scrip[illegible]s inextricably linked. Providing "first [illegible]ess (in the Scripture) and then for our weakness (in the visual display of the sacrament)," Scripture explains the sign, and the sign establishes the Scripture. The sacraments become a "mirror of spiritual blessings," which "because we have souls engrafted in bodies, he imparts spiritual things under visible ones."[28]

Calvin, ministering in a time when it had been required by the Fourth Lateran Council of 1215 that the Lord's Supper be offered only once a year, instead insisted the Supper should be celebrated "at least once a week."[29] Yet, in practice, for most of us, the sermon is the most "sacramental" of acts and the center of worship. It is the only part of the worship service in which we truly believe and fervently pray that God meets us and speaks to us. While we ask God to bless "our worship," we ask him to speak through "his Word." How different would our worship be if we prayed for Christ not only to speak to us through his Word, but also to lead us in his worship of God and meet us at his table?

While churches offer a sermon weekly, most evangelical churches celebrate the Lord's Supper, at best, monthly.[30] But in light of worship as trinitarian enactment, should that be so? Would not worship as participation be strengthened and preaching be more fully efficacious if Scripture and sacrament were more frequently and more faithfully linked together? No less an advocate for the power of the preached word then Karl Barth asks:

> Would the sermon not be delivered and listened to quite differently . . . if everything outwardly and visibly began with baptism and moved toward the Lord's Supper? Why do the numerous movements and attempts to bring the liturgy of the Reformed church up to date . . . prove without exception so unfruitful? Is it not just because they do not fix their attention on this fundamental defect, the incompleteness of our usual service, i.e., its lack of sacraments?[31]

If "the sole proper ontological basis for the church is the being of God, who is what he is as the communion of Father, Son and Spirit,"[32] then we must ask if a sermon as the center of a worship service is a faithful reflection of who God is. Isn't the corporate necessity of the sacrament that creates *communion*, requires the preached Word, and enacts *participation* a clearer reflection of the God who is Communion?[33]

Wolfhart Pannenberg goes even further to declare:

> The Eucharist, not the sermon should be the center of the church life. The religious individuality that produces itself in the pulpit . . . should not be the center of worship. The sermon should serve, not dominate in the church. It should serve the presence of Christ which we celebrate in the Eucharist.[34]

Brunner sees the sacraments as "the breakwater against the tide of individualistic enthusiasm . . . which (joins) the real and concrete congregation of the faithful in such a way as could not happen—at least so unmistakably—through the mere word of preaching."[35]

Of course, this is not to diminish the importance of the proclaimed Word, nor is it to suggest a spirituality without Scripture; indeed, the Lord's Supper *requires* the Scriptures to be read and preached.[36] It is simply to state that the individual, receptive tendencies of the sermon must always be connected to or directed toward the communal, participatory reality that is best expressed in the sacraments.[37]

At San Clemente Presbyterian Church our greatest challenges have been the logistics of trying to institute more frequent Communion services in a large congregation that currently offers three different styles of worship a week. We celebrate the Lord's Supper now every week at one of our services and monthly at all of them. Further, we have made the Lord's Supper the central activity in four additional worship services a year (Thanksgiving Eve, New Year's Eve, Ash Wednesday, Maundy Thursday) and are discussing the potential of moving toward offering regular Communion services in homes throughout the community.[38]

Ultimately, worship as participation is just another aspect of discipleship. It must always mean following the Worship Leader who "did not regard equality with God" as something to hang on to, but "emptied himself" in suffering love, the first "living sacrifice" (Phil. 2: 6; Rom. 12:1). As Torrance reminds us, participating in communion is never the end, even for the Trinity, so worship is an expression of communion with the Triune God in a "bond of mutual love and self-giving" as well as the call "to participate by the Spirit in the Son's communion with the Father and the Son's mission from the Father to the world."[39]

It is exactly this understanding of worship *as mission* that has led our San Clemente congregation to teach greeters, ushers, parking attendants, and hosts that they are not just the cookie-and-handshake crew, but are the first activity of worship led by God himself as he reaches out to the world. It means that we have gone out of our way to make our church as guest-friendly as possible. We project the words to the doxology, the Lord's Prayer, all songs, and all Scripture references on screens overhead so that a guest doesn't have to fumble with orders of service, intimidating Bibles, or unfamiliar prayers. While our three different worship services draw from a variety of styles, we intentionally use repetitive structures so that a first time guest will feel like a "regular" as soon as the second visit. Since we are expressing the triune grace of God, led by God himself in extending invitation to us, we desire for our hospitality to be a reflection of God's own.

The Offering

> God speaks, we answer. God acts, we accept and give. God gives, we receive. As a corollary to this picture, worship implies a human response in terms of *giving to God*. The theological code word for [human] offering to God is "sacrifice." The worshipper is not a pas-

sive, motionless recipient, but an active participant, called to "make an offering."[40]

Amid all the discussion of how to worship, trends in worship, and what styles we use, we sometimes forget that the earliest form of worship was to kill an animal, to offer grain, to pour out some wine. Go back to Cain and Abel and you'll recognize that long before there were prayers and songs and organs and drum sets, there was the offering. The offering is the oldest, most basic and straightforward form of worship. It is giving something to God. It is sacrificing something to demonstrate devotion and to bring pleasure to God. By the time of the temple, the worship offerings also included prayers and praise, singing and celebrating of the word. But every bit of it was judged by one single criterion: Did it please God?

Like Abel whose offering was accepted when his brother's was not, some worship is more pleasing to God than others (Gen. 4:3–5). While no reason is given for the rejection of Cain's sacrifice, we do know that Abel gave of the "firstlings of his flock, their fat portions"; that is, the very best of his flock was offered to God. The constant direction to give to God the "first fruits" reminds us that there is a "claim laid upon the worshipper to offer what is his [or her] best."[41] When we come to worship, we need to come with that spirit of offering. We need to be thinking more and more about our coming to worship as an offering of ourselves and our devotion to God.

In San Clemente we regularly encourage our congregation to "prepare" for the worship performance, as would any performer, by coming with a sense of purpose, focus, and perhaps even some preliminary study of texts and songs. While certainly we expect formal participants who sing, preach, and pray to prepare ahead of time, we often don't encourage the congregation that gathers even to prepare their hearts for a time of praise and devotion to God. If Israel was required to bring to God offerings without spot or blemish (Exod. 12:5; Lev. 14:10), should we not at least come to God with equal devotion in spirit and truth?

Certainly, some people think that anything done extemporaneously is somehow more "spiritual." Whether it is a prayer, a sermon, or even music, the lack of "preparation" is deemed as reliance upon the Spirit. We do need to be sensitive to the way that "rote liturgy" can be completely without feeling (or even thought) and that formalized orders of worship can hinder sensitivity to the Spirit in the moment. It is also easy to allow our "production value" to become an idol in trying to appease an entertainment-addicted public. However, in many settings, the lack of preparation is given a spiritual rationale for what is simply a lack of depth and effort. We must never assume that simplicity and sincerity flow easily from our usually vain and hypocritical hearts. At the very least, the concept of worship as offering suggests that preparation is a means of "giving to God the first fruits" of our energies, and doing so with sincere and prepared hearts. Worship as a performance with and for God merits preparation of the highest order.

Submissive Creative

Since Christ is the worship leader, we do well to heed the Reformers' insistence upon biblical patterns of worship that avoided "human invention."[42] Our "performance" is not an improvisational soliloquy, but submission to a divine scriptwriter, director, and leader. If nothing else, this should cause us to reflect carefully on our attempts at creativity in worship, lest we invent new forms of worship that God does not inspire or inhabit. According to Ronald Wallace, "In Calvin's view, nothing could be more dangerous to the spiritual life of the church than to open the door for the introduction of new ceremonies, however carefully calculated to appeal to the worshipper."[43] In his commentary on Jesus' words to the Samaritan woman, "You worship what you know not, we worship what we know," Calvin states:

> This is a sentence worthy of being remembered, and teaches us that we ought not to attempt anything in religion rashly or at random, unless there be knowledge, it is not God we worship but a phantom or an idol. All good intentions, as they are called, are struck by this sentence as a thunderbolt; for we learn from it that [people] can do nothing but err, where they are guided by their own opinion without the Word or command of God.[44]

This is not necessarily meant to criticize everything "contemporary" (indeed the Reformers were able "contemporizers," and our church in San Clemente is far more contemporary than most) but instead to challenge worship that is innovative for the sake of innovation (or even traditional for the sake of being traditional!). Old notes that while Calvin does not speak out against the writing of Psalms or the use of musical instruments, an oft-repeated comment, he also repeatedly makes the point that the "liturgy is not the place to express our own human creativity. The Christian is not to go about inventing new forms of worship, but rather as a matter of the obedience of faith, Christians are to worship according to God's Word."[45]

In our church, this doesn't mean that we don't try to be imaginative. But we also don't place too much weight on "appealing to the worshiper." While we do everything possible to offer hospitality to our guests as an expression of God's gracious invitation, we expressly do not encourage people to sit back and observe. Quite the opposite: we pick songs, Scripture texts, and prayers that are meant to enable everyone regardless of age or maturity in faith to give themselves to God fully and authentically. We intentionally use Scripture as the focal point for our worshipers, centering moments of reflection, musical interludes, and prayers with Scripture passages projected on the screens at the front of the Sanctuary.

Not insignificantly, on the other end of the style spectrum, in Isaiah, "human commandment" is decried as any action "learned by rote" that attempts to honor God with mouths alone while "their hearts are far from me" (Isa. 29:13–14).[46] From this, it is obvious that any forms—from the most high church to the most seeker-sensitive—can fall into the trap of being "mere" human invention.

Perhaps most important for this discussion, however, are the practices of the Reformers as they instituted what they called worship "according to the Scriptures." They not only exhorted worshipers to "incline their hearts" and worship God in truth in Jesus Christ, but they also undertook a program of "adaptation and education,"[47] where traditional forms were "corrected to convey biblical meanings."

The Reformers adapted traditional forms to their own cultural contexts and labored to nurture the ability of all people to "unite themselves to voice the sung and spoken prayers of the service." Since all believers are priests, whose prayers and praises are a "sacrifice" to God, then the forms of worship must be understandable and accessible.

> One could not really expect the whole congregation to sing what the trained monastic choirs had been singing, nor could one simply translate the Latin texts into German or French and sing the new text to old music. Besides that the taste in music was changing rapidly . . . the Reformation was amazingly successful in refreshing the praises of the church.[48]

Nichols points out that Calvin discusses church music under the heading of prayer[49] where, again, the goal is the whole participation of the people of God in worship and mutual edification. In Calvin's liturgy, people often sang responses to spoken prayers with simple tunes that facilitated a focusing upon the written word and not simply the aesthetics of music. Calvin warned that "our ears be not more attentive to the melody than our minds to the spiritual meanings of words." The intended goal is full, heartfelt participation by the whole people of God as an offering to God, an offering that shows the world just what God is worth.

The Secret of Transforming Worship

A couple of years ago, our church was visited by the worship committees of a couple of churches who wanted to observe our growing multigenerational services. One group came to our 11:00 praise-band-led worship, and I remember it being a particularly moving service. Our worship director had designed a brilliant service, our musicians played seamlessly with the band, their third service of three different sets of music that day. Our vocal team consisted of our middle-aged choir director and a college woman, joyfully demonstrating the true passion they have for multigenerational worship. The junior high students kept standing up and singing their hearts out; the rest of us clapped along enthusiastically with the relatively limited amount of rhythm we have. It was a wonderful service where we could sense God's presence and were so deeply aware of the great joy that comes when we all together give ourselves to God.

As soon as the service was over, some members of the visiting church's worship committee asked if their pastor could ask me some questions about how we got to this place in our worship. I said,

"Sure. I don't know what I'll tell him, but ask away." When the pastor walked up to me he had only one question: "So, what did you pay for those screens?"

If my momma had not raised me to be polite, I would have yelled in his face. "Screens? You think this is about screens? This is about an entire church that believes that we are here to *give ourselves*—all of ourselves, every one of ourselves, from baby to senior—*to God* in worship. You want to ask me about the screens? This is about the people. It is about our worship director spending three years on Saturday nights learning how to lead worship for a new generation. It is about our choir director spending ten years training every choir in this church to be a group of worship leaders, including the bell and children's choirs. It is about the entire youth department changing its focus on Sunday morning so that every child and youth can be part of the worship life of the church and not just have a kids' program where they never darken the doors of the sanctuary. It's about people who are more interested in the encounter with God offered every morning in the Lord's Supper than about sleeping in an extra hour. It's about a group of older worshipers who are more concerned about the glory of God being demonstrated to a watching world than getting their musical preferences. And all you want to know is how much the *screens* cost?"

Of course, that is what I *wanted* to say.

What I said was, "About $30,000, given to us through the estate of one of our oldest members when she went to glory, because she loved to see children worship and grow in Christ."

I can just imagine that pastor going back to his session: "You know, the secret of San Clemente Presbyterian Church is that they have great big screens." That's a shame. Our worship is no more about our screens than it is about our organ or our electronic drum set. We could show up next week in the parking lot under a canvas tent, and we'd still worship God, because the secret of our worship is that we know that we are called to perform for God in front of a watching world. We are called to give glory to the Triune God in all the earth. God has commanded it, we enjoy it, and it is our pleasure to offer it.

8

Transforming Word I

Look, Listen, Live!

A young Jewish couple has a baby boy and visits their rabbi to ask for help. Being devout, the couple desperately wants to raise their son according to God's will for his life. They ask the rabbi, "How can we know what God's will is for our son?"

The rabbi says, "Here's what I want you to do. When you get home tonight, go into one of the rooms in the house and clear everything out of the room except for one table. On the table I want to you put a bottle of Scotch whiskey, a roll of dollar bills, and a copy of the Scriptures. Then leave the room and leave the child in the room with those three things." The young couple nods but looks puzzled.

The rabbi continues. "If your boy grabs the Scotch whiskey, he's going to grow up and be a drunk. If he grabs the money, he's going to grow up and go into business. But if he grabs the Scriptures, then he'll be a rabbi."

The next day the couple comes back and says, "Rabbi, we have to talk to you. We're totally confused; we don't know what to do. We did exactly what you said, we put the child in a room and on the table we put Scotch whiskey, a roll of money, and the Scriptures and then went out of the room.

"We peeked inside and watched as he immediately went over and grabbed the Scotch whiskey and took a huge drink. Then he grabbed the money and shoved it in his pocket, and then he picked up the Scriptures and has not stopped reading it. What does this mean?"

The rabbi said "Oh, I've got very, very, bad news for you. Your son is going to grow up to be . . . a Presbyterian."

As a Presbyterian pastor, I tell that story anytime I visit a new church (especially a Presbyterian one!). I want to remind my brothers and sisters that no matter what our foibles—whether we're accused of moral laxity or being overly worldly—we are people of the Book. Indeed, especially we evangelicals are boldly and unabashedly committed to teaching and studying the Word of God. But it is worth asking, Is being biblical enough?

We live in a world today in which you can get the Bible twenty-four hours a day; you can have it on tapes, CDs, and on the Internet; you can listen to it through headsets; you can read it in every version or format imaginable. You can get a men's version, a women's version, a kids' version, a teenage version. You can get a version that takes you through "the prayer of Jabez" or a version that gives you affirmations for losing weight.

You can have a Bible that answers all your questions or a Bible that is easy to take on the go. There are more Bibles today than ever. And if that's not enough, a biblically based sermon is only as far away as your tape player, CD player, web browser, TV, or radio.

Consider how different this is than in the first century, when the only Scriptures people had were the Old Testament and the stories of Jesus that the apostles told and the church repeated. For hundreds of years, nobody had his or her own Bible in his or her native language. Bibles were read only in the midst of worship services and usually in a language that most people wouldn't have understood.

Eventually, and wonderfully, Bibles were translated into common languages and then made widely accessible because of the invention of movable type. With every new medium of communication, then, the Word of God is dispersed more and more. In a way that Guttenberg and Wycliffe could never have imagined, the seed of the Scripture is scattered to every corner of the globe.

Yet with all this information so available, with the word of God "that never returns void" so powerful, why aren't we more noticeably different from the world around us? Speaking in 1993, Dallas Willard voiced a disturbing observation:

> We [evangelicals] have counted on preaching and teaching to form faith in the hearer, and on faith to form the inner life and ordered behavior of the Christian. But, for whatever reason, this strategy has not turned out well. The result is that we have multitudes of professing Christians that well may be ready to die, but obviously are not ready to live, and can hardly get along with themselves, much less others.[1]

From the responses, virtually all in attendance agreed with Willard's assessment: Christians assume that being "biblical" will result in being sanctified, and yet that assumption seems highly questionable at best. This is, of course, a serious problem. Our theology asserts that personal sanctification is the work of the Spirit bringing the Christian into conformity with Christ through the inward application of the Scriptures.[2] Yet, if Willard is correct, then despite a commitment to the Scriptures, this is exactly what is not happening.[3]

How does Christ, through the Spirit, effect change? The traditional answer is: through the Scriptures; through the preaching, reading, studying, and, some would say, memorizing of the Scriptures. The Word of God (written in Scripture, proclaimed in preaching, experienced in sacraments) creates faith in the hearer, regenerating and transforming the believer through the power of God (Rom. 1:16–17, 10:8–10, 17; Eph. 1:13). With David, we are encouraged to "treasure" God's word "in our hearts" so that we might not sin against God (Ps. 119:11). The Scriptures "lay bare" the human heart, revealing all that is true about our divided loyalties and defensive denial, our sinful attitudes and our confused motivations (Heb. 4:12). The Scriptures also teach, correct, reproof, and train us, so that we are "equipped for every good work" (2 Tim. 3:16–17). They serve as both the Surgeon's scalpel and the Renovator's hammer, cutting away what is spiritually diseased and harmful and building up what is divinely beneficial and consistent.

Yet, as Dallas Willard and others have demonstrated, the Scriptures have often been disturbingly ineffective in bringing about this transformation. Could it be that it is the *use* of the Scriptures that needs to be reexamined?[4]

So it is worth asking some seemingly obvious question: *What is the Bible anyway?* Is it a collection of eternal truths wrapped in cultural garb that need to be disrobed and deciphered? Or is it instead a compendium of facts about times and places, beliefs and behaviors that need to be declared and defended? Traditionally, "liberal" interpreters have preferred the first vision, and more "conservative" commentators have insisted on the latter. But are either of these options what the Bible is intended to be?[5]

Another question: *How are we to read it?* Is it meant to be picked apart and dissected into nuances of word meanings and grammatical devices? Or is it meant to be searched for the spiritual meaning locked away in ordinary words? Traditionally, "scholarly" students using higher criticism preferred the former, and "spiritual" searchers preferred the latter. But are they mutually exclusive? And in all cases, the assumption, of course, is that the goal of Bible reading is *understanding*, and the reader reads *alone*.

In this chapter I want to suggest a different way of reading the Scriptures. It is not a new approach; in fact it is the oldest. It is the approach of the Hebrews at the Passover, and Jesus at the Last Supper. It is the approach of the earliest Christians in the very first "church service," and it is the approach of the Puritans. We want to learn how to read the Scriptures as I believe they would be read in the divine communion. And to recover this way of reading requires asking two questions: How? Where?

> How do we read the Scriptures? *As a performative document.*
> Where do we read them? *At dinner time.*
> *We need to read the Scriptures as a recipe and at a meal.*

But before we turn to those questions, we need to spend a little time reviewing the whole concept of the Word of God. In the sections that follow, I will show how the doctrine of the threefold Word of God leads to a trinitarian approach to the Word that is necessary for formation. Second, I will describe a trinitarian approach to Scripture that reveals it as the *icon of the grace of the Son, the story of the love of the Father, and the wisdom of the communion of the Spirit* for the express purpose of being performed in a life-transforming way. Third, I will demonstrate that the Bible is most powerful when read within a community as a shared discipline expressed through Scripture and sacrament.

Bigger than the Bible: The Trinitarian Word of God

As we have seen, a central concept of the work and nature of the Trinity is the interrelatedness, or perichoresis, of the persons of the Trinity. In the salvific encounter with God, we experience the presence of the one God in the different persons of the Trinity and therefore come to understand that the God we encounter is Triune. This trinitarian encounter is not only the description of God, but also the description of God's Word. Traditionally put forth as the "threefold Word of God,"[6] it reminds us that God's self-communication is heard ultimately in the Word, or Logos, Jesus Christ. Since Jesus is the Trinity's expression, the Word of God is then always and simultaneously

1. the eternal Logos of God *incarnate* (the Word in the flesh as Jesus the person),[7]
2. the voice of *inspiration* in the biblical Word given to and standing over the church[8] (the Word written in Scripture),[9]
3. the light of *illumination* in the Word of God proclaimed within the Community of God (the Word preached).[10]

This threefold presence of Christ operates perichoretically through each expression of the Word of God, so that Jesus Christ himself is present as God incarnate, conceived by the Holy Spirit; God's Word in Scriptures inspired by the Holy Spirit; and God's Word proclaimed, illuminated by the Holy Spirit. This leads to a trinitarian approach to reading the Scriptures.

As we will see, the sacraments as *verbum visible, verbum communale* also have this threefold pattern: as the visual word proclaiming Christ "until he comes" (1 Cor. 11:26), the enacted word remembering the Word, Jesus (1 Cor. 11:24–25), and the communal word of the participation in Christ of the people of God (1 Cor. 10:16). In short, Scripture and sacrament are Jesus' personal encountering presence:

calling, guiding, empowering, and transforming the believer into the image of God seen in him, the Word of God.

The community of Christ is, therefore, the community of the Word in its threefold pattern revealed through Scripture and sacrament. The Word is incarnate, written, and proclaimed—both individually and communally, both verbally and visually. The presence, the stories, and the symbols all together transform perichoretically in a trinitarian pattern. God is present (though veiled) in the Scripture and signs. The Scriptures as divine stories of God reveal the presence and then ensure that the signs are revelatory. The signs of God make tangible both the stories and the Spirit. And the stories and signs together bring about the calling, confronting, empowering, guiding, and, ultimately, transforming of the believer and the community.

But how do these divine stories and signs transform? By calling us to God in revelation, by commanding and instructing us in the ways of God, and by strengthening and nourishing us to hear, to heed the command, and to obey the instructions. Through the Word, the Spirit so cultivates the union of wills, so reveals the knowledge of God, so guides the responsive actions that we become more and more transformed in heart, mind, and walk, if we use the Scripture for its divine purpose and in the manner that is commanded to us. In short, if the Bible is a recipe, then it is best read at a meal.

The Recipe for Transformation: Look, Listen, and Live

My wife loves to read recipes. Beth has two or three magazines that appear in our mailbox every month just loaded with pictures and descriptions of the most mouth-watering meals imaginable. Every now and then, she'll read one aloud to me, and by the time she is done, I am so hungry I want to lick the magazine. Fortunately for me, Beth is a fabulous cook, and so eventually the recipe that she read will result in a delicious meal for me.

But what if all Beth ever did was read the recipes? What if she never cooked the meal? Most would agree that the purpose of a recipe is not merely to be read, but to produce something. It is not just words for understanding, but words to be "performed."

According to Nicholas Lash, this is exactly the way the Bible is to be understood. "The fundamental form of the Christian interpretation of scripture is the performance of the biblical text."[11] Lash compares Scripture to a musical score (which is to be performed) or the U.S. Constitution (which is to be enacted). I have a friend who has a portion of an ancient musical score framed in his home on the wall. It's beautiful. It is written in stunning calligraphy and color. Looking at it, you can't help but be impressed by its beauty. But is that musical score doing what it's supposed to be doing, framed on that wall? No. A score is not being put to use until it is sung or played.

Consider also the Constitution of the United States. Have you ever stood in line in Washington, D.C., to see the original Constitution? It is indeed a marvelous sight to behold and stirs feelings of patriotism and nostalgia. But is that all it's supposed to do? What's the purpose of that grand document? It's to be thumbed over, read, learned, and legislated. We're supposed to live by it and order our society by it.

These documents—Constitution, score, or recipe—are not doing their purpose until they are performed. And that's true of the Bible also. The Bible accomplishes nothing until it is lived out. It's a performative document.

Scripture is then interpreted "correctly," not if it corresponds to some objective reality (whether the "eternal truths" of liberals or the "factual referent" of conservatives), but if it leads to faithful action by a community of God's people. Exegetical work and devotional attention are not completed until the Scripture is embodied in a community of believers in a way that is consistent with the community's commitment to the lordship of Jesus Christ.[12]

Scripture even says this about itself; 2 Timothy 3:16–17: "All scripture is inspired by God and is useful for teaching, for reproof, for correction, and for training in righteousness, so that everyone who belongs to God may be proficient, equipped for every good work." Notice how practical a definition that is. The Bible says that the purpose of Scripture is to be useful. Also notice what Scripture is not. The verse says that it is inspired, but that doesn't mean that it's necessarily inspiring.

Scripture is not high art; it doesn't necessarily move the soul to spiritual visions or awe-inspiring acts of obedience. Oh, it can at times, and I am amazed when it does. Every time I perform a wedding I am a little stunned when the couple asks for 1 Corinthians 13 to be read. It is not a romantic love poem. It's not Dickinson, or Shakespeare, or Browning; it's not even the Song of Solomon. It's not "How do I love thee, let me count the ways." It's "Love is patient; love is kind; love is not envious or boastful or arrogant or rude. . . . It bears all things . . . endures all things."

Writers have penned many words more beautiful and inspiring than "love bears all things." Nevertheless, we want it read at our weddings. Why is that? Because part of us knows that there's enough emotion in the room already and that we need to be reminded of what true love is and what marriages requires. Amid all wedding sentimentality, 1 Corinthians 13 is read so that we will remember it after the wedding, when we need to be reminded that love is going to endure all things, including you.

The purpose of the Scripture is to be useful: to teach, to correct or guide, to train and equip people to live well. So how best do we use it? How best do we put the recipe to work and make something that nourishes and strengthens us? Let me suggest a trinitarian pattern for reading and performing the word based upon some simple directions: Look, listen, and live!

Look! Scripture as the *Icon* of the Grace of the Son

> I will seek Thee, Lord, by calling on Thee; and will call on Thee, believing in Thee; for to us hast Thou been preached. My faith, Lord, shall call on Thee, which Thou hast given me, wherewith Thou hast inspired me, through the Incarnation of Thy Son, through the ministry of the Preacher.[13]

In *The Confessions,* Augustine gives us a classic description of spiritual formation. He seeks God because Christ has been preached. The Word of God comes to us, brings about the change of heart that inspires the seeking of God. It is a divine encounter where God is "enfleshed" in human words, "a veiling of himself in order to reveal himself";[14] an epiphany of God's very presence, "face-to-face."[15]

John Calvin believed that the Scriptures are the spectacles of the Spirit,[16] a set of eyeglasses for overcoming the nearsightedness of human sinfulness. As such, the first way of using the Scriptures is to look through them, not at them. Now, I don't wear eyeglasses, but I live in a beach town where the sun is wonderfully bright and where sunglasses are practically required equipment. When you wear glasses, you don't look at them unless something is wrong. A bug or a smudge gets on the lens, and you take them off to examine them. But otherwise, when all is working properly, you look through them so that you can see what is around you.

Calvin said that without the Scriptures we're all nearsighted; while we certainly can see some things about reality, because of our sinfulness we won't see reality accurately until we have the Scriptures as the corrective lens bringing focus and cutting the glare.

I think about this whenever I go snorkeling. If you stick your head underwater without a mask, all you can see are murky and fuzzy images. You certainly can make out some things, but not accurately. But put on a mask or set of goggles, and immediately everything is clear.

Without the Bible we can certainly look at the world and see much evidence for a Creator, we can read history and hear about a religious figure who started a movement and died on a cross, we can see people going to church and acknowledge the power of ideas. But only through the lens of the Scriptures do we see that the Creator came to earth, that God was on the cross, that the carpenter who died as a scandal was saving the world. The Scriptures give us the lens by which to see.

In the Scriptures, the Word serves as an "icon" of God's own presence, a revelation of God behind the "veil" of human words, an incarnational moment where words become Word, where symbols become signs. Some may object to my use of the term *icon*. But, indeed, if we understand the purpose of the icon within Eastern Orthodoxy, we recognize that Scripture has the same revealing-while-veiling quality as an icon. According to the late Leonid Ouspensky, one of the greatest iconographers and iconologists of his time,[17] the theology of the icon is tied to the incarnation.

The icon expresses the incomprehensible God becoming comprehensible by taking on human flesh. In the incarnation, God condescends to be described, to be limited (as a human), and to be defined (in human terms): the icon seeks to express this reality by portraying the God-man as a human who has been glorified. It depicts the reality of the glory and humiliation of God in Christ, simultaneously.[18] To the Eastern Orthodox, this "double-reality" of the divine presence and the human form is parallel to Scripture. In the ordinary words of the human preacher (which are "mere words") there is some other presence or reality that is beyond words, the encounter of the divine presence and power.[19]

Calvin uses for Scripture the same incarnation language that is used for Christ himself in John 1: "The glory of God so shines in His Word" revealing God "as though he were nigh to us, face to face."[20] The preached and read Scriptures within the community of faith have a kind of holiness that other words do not have, yet they are "just words." The Word is a "sign,"[21] a "mirror" reflecting the very glory of God,[22] and the very Word of God,[23] at the same time. Like the icon's depiction of Jesus, the Scriptures offer an "encountering" quality, which creates the very reality they proclaim.[24]

As an Orthodox believer looks through an icon to gain a transforming glimpse into the spiritual realm, so the Word offers a transforming glimpse of the presence of God "veiled" in the human words.[25] The Word is not merely a referent to or a reminder of an objective "eternal truth" or historic event; it is itself the vital encounter with the living God whose power transforms (Rom. 1:16). The Spirit causes an effectual union between Christ and the believer through faith in the hearing of the gospel and cultivates that union through the sacraments.[26] The Word is the means to a genuine face-to-face interaction with God; a transforming encounter where God is powerfully present.

> First, the Lord teaches and instructs us by his Word. Secondly, he confirms it by the sacraments. Finally he illumines our hearts for the Word and sacraments to enter in, which would otherwise only strike our ears and appear before our eyes, but not at all affect within.[27]

As the icon of God in Christ, the Scriptures are first something to look through and see what we could never see in our fallenness: the grace of the Triune God reaching into human history and every human heart, inviting each soul into Divine Communion. But as a trinitarian Word that operates perichoretically, not only is it the icon that shows us the grace of the Son, but it is, at the same time, the story of the divine love of the Father.

Listen! Scripture as the *Story* of the Love of the Father

> Apart from being a good story, the narrative becomes to those who read it as believers (united in the Holy Spirit to the Lord Jesus) a personal communication. In fact, Christians are wholly involved in this story because they are brought into union with the Father, through the Son and in the Holy Spirit. The story, which is ultimately the story of the Holy Trinity, becomes their story. They are involved in divine autobiography.[28]

The idea of faith as connected to "narrative" is a popular postmodern idea. *Narrative* refers to a method of presenting and patterning Christian belief according to its "linear development from creation to consummation."[29] This is not an artificial construct that realigns the use of Scripture, but a method inspired by Scripture itself. As New Testament scholar N. T. Wright has written, "the early Christians were story-tellers . . . stories were visibly and obviously an essential part of what they were and did."[30] As such, story-telling and living out the story of Christ are not only the Book of Acts but the life of the church today. As my former senior pastor, Lloyd Ogilvie, used to say, "the Book of Acts continues today."

In the movie *The Dead Poets Society,* Robin Williams plays a teacher, Mr. Keating, who quotes Walt Whitman to his students, all adolescent boys: "'The powerful play goes on, and you can contribute a verse.' What will your verse be, boys?" To read the Scripture as a performative document means that not only do we look through it to see the grace of Christ coming to and calling us, but we also listen to it as a divine narrative; a story that we are to act out. It is a story that involves us and insists that we enter it.

Divine narrative is the Spirit's Word that transforms through story, language, and symbol. It involves encounter and gradual change. The experience of God who is revealed within the history, recapitulated in the stories, and reenacted in the sacraments of the people of God is a reality that is evident throughout the Bible. Whether it is the refugees from the exile telling the creation and ancestral stories of the

God of Abraham, Isaac, and Jacob, the old psalms used by Christians to form their understanding of their risen Lord, the stories of Jesus that become the basis of the Scriptures, or the clear catechizing of a mixed-race new covenant people with the old covenant stories of their new, adopted family history,[31] the narrative of the divine love of the Father shapes the people of God through stories and symbols, language and worldview. Transformation takes place as the narrative of the Christian community becomes the history of their identity, a present encounter, and the future path as they journey together with God.

But, once again, this is a story to be performed. According to Gabriel Fackre, believers "are formed by that faith only as we are engaged by its narrative form."[32] Not only does the narrative communicate content but the story itself transforms. Jesus' own storytelling sought to "[break] open the worldview of Jesus' hearers, so that it could be remolded into the worldview which he, Jesus, was commending."[33] As we read the story by which we define ourselves as Christians, the "jars and jolts" of the story "reorient" us and encourage a confrontation between the way we are living and the values and intentions of the story.[34] "The result is a narrative in which the readers are caught up in the world of the text and transformed by it."[35]

> Far from seeking, like Homer, merely to make us forget our own reality for a few hours, [biblical narrative] seeks to overcome our reality; we are to fit our own life into its world, feel ourselves to be elements in its structure of universal history.[36]

However, for Christians, the central, reality-overcoming, life-restructuring idea is not the form of the narrative, but its content, that is, the story of the divine love of the Father in Jesus Christ. The engagement that transforms is not just any story, but specifically, the story of Jesus.[37] Only in the gospel do we find the "story" of God as a loving Father, because we know the Father only through the Son (John 14:9, 21). A trinitarian, narrative approach to the Scriptures affirms that the "center" of faith, the "revelatory hinge" of God's history and the only "full and true knowledge of God" (John 1:17–18) is in Jesus Christ.[38]

As believers begin to learn the story of Jesus, it becomes the "script" of their lives, leading to a new pattern of living. The believers start to become *(de facto)* what they are *(de jure)*. This is exactly Paul's mode of ethical instruction, encouraging the Corinthians to understand that in their behavior they were acting not according the new story of their identity as believers but according to the old "script" of who they were.

> Do you not know that wrongdoers will not inherit the kingdom of God? Do not be deceived! Fornicators, idolaters, adulterers, male prostitutes, sodomites, thieves, the greedy, drunkards, revilers, robbers—none of these will inherit the kingdom of God. *And this is what some of you used to be*. But you were washed, you were sanctified, you were justified in the name of the Lord Jesus Christ and in the Spirit of our God. (1 Cor. 6:9–11, emphasis mine)

They who have been called "holy" by divine imputation now gradually become holy through transformation. The story and the Spirit who inspired the story, when heard and heeded, transform.

Miroslav Volf reminds us that for stories to truly transform, they must be far more than just content communicated, even the content of the divine love of the Father in Jesus, and must include the personal and experiential way in which that content is communicated.

> Think of the stories at bedside and the radiance of a face reflecting the love of Christ, words of admonition and the silent holding of the hand of a person in pain, eating and drinking the bread and wine, worship of the one true God, holiness and failure, manipulation and sword, the blood of the martyrs, the lives of the saints, hypocrisy and lust for power among church dignitaries and the rest of us, and economic interests and political machinations.[39]

This means that *who* reads the Biblical stories and *how* they are read are as important as the fact that they are read. Christian education is therefore always a combination of the content and the communicator. Again, while content is ubiquitous, true loving teachers of the Scriptures must continually be called forth.

In my congregation, that means that while we will certainly take advantage of the technological advantages of video curricula, sermon tapes, and Christian books, our emphasis is on developing teachers, small-group leaders, and individual disciplers to personally, lovingly, and accurately pass on the faith. My own children have seen "The Jesus Film" and many *Veggie Tales* cartoons, but they have also learned their faith through the lilting Scottish brogue of a seventy-year-old Sunday school teacher, the teenage vacation bible school leader who made Christianity seem "cool," the sparkling eyes of their "spiritual grandparents," who pray for them every day, and the hands of their parents, who stroke their heads and sing them off-key praise songs to put them to bed at night.

This blend of experiential and personal dimensions and the actual content also points, once again, to the necessity for the community to connect its stories to the sacraments. The divine narrative is always "enacted" within the community of faith like holy stories around a family dinner table. The sacraments serve as a family connecting point and enactment of the story in their inclusion of new members through the washing of baptism or the nourishing of the Supper. Indeed, Wright reminds us that the first Christians functioned as an "alternative family," a new sociopolitical reality that recast one's involvement in every other group. "The early church was thus marked out from the first as a familial community, loyalty to which overrode all other considerations."[40]

For the Scripture to be performed, we first *look* through it to see the grace of Jesus initiating the journey with the call to follow. We also listen to the *stories* of the divine love of the Father revealed in Jesus as a kind of "map." However, more than just an invitation and description, more than an inspiration and a sign, is necessary. To successfully follow Christ in the "way of salvation," the pilgrim needs not only invitation and inspiration, but also instruction; not only description and signs, but wisdom.

Live! Scripture as the *Wisdom* of the Spirit

In Luke, chapter 3, John the Baptist comes out of the wilderness quoting from Isaiah. Using the narratives of the very people he was addressing, he goes from painting a verbal picture of the way of salvation for all flesh to a harsh criticism of the complacency of those who believed that their lineage made them exempt from the need for repentance. The crowd, convicted, openhearted, and responsive to a change of life, asks, "What shall we do?" John lays out some specifics, and the crowd marvels, wondering aloud whether they have seen the Messiah.

In our context, John is an iconic experience of the Old Testament prophet Isaiah and the God that Isaiah revealed, calling people to respond to the new reality of God. John tells the narrative of the people of God and connects to their own stories by revealing the gap between their lives and the new reality. Then, he offers practical wisdom. This vignette serves as a good type of the work of the Trinity through the Scriptures: from communal calling experience, through communal guiding narrative, to communal faithful action, each transforming—yet together—perichoretically. That is, all participate in the transforming encounter, story, and wisdom: narratives have a wisdom, iconic words have a story, and wisdom is based on a story and an experience.

It is tempting to end the discussion here; to speak of encounter and the story and leave it to each person to work out how they respond accordingly. In fact, most spiritual seekers today seem to do just that: claiming the symbols of Christ and the stories of God and then living them out as they see fit. According to the Scripture, however, the encounter has not occurred and the story has not been heard until both are embodied in a community. That embodiment is the work of the Spirit teaching believers how to live after the pattern of Christ (Gal. 5:16–17).[41]

Stanley Hauerwas reminds us that "What ought I to do?" (to live by the Spirit of Christ) is always and—necessarily—subsequent to "What are we or ought we to be?" (as the community of the Spirit of Christ). The ethical question concerning right action is subsequent to descriptions of communal identity and the authoritative guiding story.[42] Prohibitions serve as the "markers of the outer limits" of the community's self-understanding. "In short, they tell us that if we do this or no longer disapprove of that, we will no longer be living out the tradition that originally formed us."[43]

My friend and former colleague Tony Osimo once told about how he and his wife, Anne, disciplined his young son. He said that when he once caught the boy teasing his younger sister, Tony sat him down and said, "Son, we Osimos respect people. We Osimos are kind and protective of those who are younger than us. We Osimos are loving and gentle with each other."

What Tony was doing was not only correcting his son's behavior, but also connecting his behavior to his family identity. He was at once teaching values and reminding his son that he too is loved, belongs to a family, and is expected to live out the family's values. In the same way Jesus defined his community in familial terms—mother and brothers—as a community of wisdom: those who practically live out the Word (Luke 8:21). The true community of Christ is the community who is blessed because they live wisely: hearing the word and doing it (James 1:22–25). For Calvin, a "strict adherence to the word constitutes spiritual chastity."[44]

Theologically, ethical wisdom is always connected to the work of the Spirit, which is linked traditionally to Calvin's *tertius usus legius*. Calvin describes this "third use of the law" as the Lord instructing, "by their reading of it those whom he inwardly instills with a readiness to obey."[45] This "third use of the law" is the principal use that "finds its place among believers among whose proper hearts the Spirit of God already lives and reigns." We lay "hold not only of the precepts but, the accompanying promise of grace," which according to the Heidelberg Catechism both "assures me of eternal life, and makes me wholeheartedly willing and ready from now on to live for him."[46] Indeed, at the end of the section on the Ten Commandments, we are reminded that even the Decalogue is preached so that "we may constantly and diligently pray to God for the grace of the Holy Spirit, so that more and more we may be renewed in the image of God, until we attain the goal of full perfection after this life."[47]

Wisdom is living out the law of God written on our hearts (Jer. 31–33) from the wellspring and security of the new life of the Spirit. It is the community's faithful response to the encounter of the word of Christ and the story of the love of the Father. It is the guidance given to the community for daily obedience and continual conformation of its life through the internal presence of Christ's Spirit. For Calvin, the written word is the guide for the church. "When it pleased God to raise up a more visible form of a church it was his will that his word should be committed to writing, that his priests might seek from it what to teach people, and that every doctrine to be taught should conform to that rule."[48]

So we now realize that the Scripture is a performative document, a recipe. For the Scriptures to, in fact, serve as the primary instrument for spiritual formation, the community of faith must have an approach to them grounded in the reality of the threefold Word of God. The Scriptures, if they are to be effective in spiritual formation, must be performed within the community as the encountering icon of Christ, the story of the love of the Father, and the wisdom of the Spirit.

To see the Word of Scripture and sacrament as icon is to believe that God is present in an incarnational way; coming to us in the manner of Jesus. The very face of God is present in the Scriptures, the very encounter we need is present to us. Like an icon that reveals God's presence, the Word is a window to another "world," which challenges us to live before a greater reality and live out our eternal and abundant life here. Therefore, the Word operates in the same way as Jesus' very presence: an announcement of, an encounter with, and an invitation to the reign of God.

To see the Word of Scripture and sacrament as a story is to believe that God is present in a historical and self-defining way: coming to us in God's loving promises and actions demonstrated in Israel, embodied in Jesus, and passed down to the church. Biblical narratives reveal to us the content, the history, and the ethics of the kingdom, providing both a context for our lives and a challenge to our living. We are changed as we live out the story of God within the story of the present world.

To see the Word of Scripture and sacrament as wisdom is to believe that God is with us in an authoritative, guiding way, giving us both the inspiration and the instruction of the Spirit to follow the way of Jesus in discipleship. Wisdom is living out the law of God from the wellspring and security of the new life of the Spirit. It is living out the new law written on our hearts, responding to the presence of God in increasing, spiritually inspired conformity of life and action.

However, even if the Scriptures are now "seen" in this trinitarian way, to see is not necessarily to change. For that, new practices are necessary, beginning with where we read the Scriptures. If we want the Word to truly change us, it is not enough to rightly read the recipe; we must also place it back in their proper context for study and application, the church community. The recipe must lead to a meal.

9

Transforming Word II

Reading at the Table

When I first decided to consciously follow Christ, I was told to read the Bible. It was and remains essential and exceedingly helpful advice. But what that usually meant was that I was to read the Bible *by myself*. Of course, I was encouraged to go to Bible study and certainly exhorted to listen to sermons. But mostly I was told that growing in Christ would depend upon my faithfulness to having a "quiet time."

Citing Psalm 5:3 "My voice shalt thou hear in the morning, O Lord; in the morning will I direct my prayer unto thee, and will look up" (KJV), I was told that to be a growing Christian would require me to get up early, read the Bible, and pray. This is, of course, perfectly fine advice. But what is significant is what verse is overlooked.

In Acts 2 we are told of the first believers who heard Peter's message of the crucified and risen Lord. In verse 37 we are told that the crowd asked Peter and the disciples, "Brothers, what should we do?" Peter responded, "Repent and be baptized" (v. 38). In other words, change their minds about who Christ is and join the community who follows him. Then, in verses 42 and 46–47, we are told of the earliest believers:

> They devoted themselves to the apostles' teaching and fellowship, to the breaking of bread and the prayers. . . . Day by day, as they spent much time together in the temple, they broke bread at home and ate their food with glad and generous hearts, praising God and having the goodwill of all the people. And day by day the Lord added to their number those who were being saved.

Notice that the first priority for living out the new-found faith was to join a supper club. The early church was primarily a body of people who gathered regularly to eat, learn, love, and pray together. If the purpose of the Bible is to perform it, then the place to perform it is in the community where God is personally and powerfully present in a life-transforming way. If the Bible is a recipe, then the Bible is read most effectively when it *constitutes* a meal.

In our church we have taken this passage very seriously and are building our entire Christian education program around meals. In fact, we are in the middle of an $8 million building program that will renovate our entire church campus for the express purpose of being able to bring the whole church together once a week for a dinner and then various educational classes by age, stage, and interest. Our small group leaders are all taught not only how to lead Bible discussions, but also how to build the discussions around meals together to deepen the fellowship and to better enact the Acts 2:42 model. Our dream is to someday have a Bible study available in every one of our neighborhoods[1] and to offer regular home communion gatherings led by elders and deacons in every neighborhood, so that the Lord's Table will be a regular part of every Christian's life.

According to 2 Corinthians 3:18, believers are transformed by seeing the glory of the Lord (that is, the face of Christ revealed in the gospel) as the reflection of God.[2]

> And all of us, with unveiled faces, seeing the glory of the Lord as though reflected in a mirror, are being transformed into the same image from one degree of glory to another; for this comes from the Lord, the Spirit.

But if one were to ask, "How does a person see the glory of the Lord as though reflected in a mirror?" Calvin, expounding on 2 Corinthians 3:18, would answer, "Through the Word and sacraments."[3]

In his commentary on the passage he writes, "Let us not be ashamed to give this honor to his Word and sacrament—to behold him there is face-to-face." This leads us to then agree with Nicholas Lash, who asserts that the "performance of the biblical text" is "best illustrated in the celebration of the Eucharist," where the story is told "not just to be relished or remembered" but that it may express a following of Jesus, a sharing or participating in the life and ministry of Christ.[4]

Again, crucial to understand here is the classic notion that the sacraments are themselves understood to be the "Word of God," made visible, active and communal.[5] Further, the "sacraments properly administered" always include the reading and preaching of the Scriptures. In fact, the Scriptures and the sacrament need each other if the Word is to be fully comprehended and God's people are to be fully transformed. The sacraments are the visible, communal and active word of the encounter, the enacted word of the narratives, and the empowering, energizing word for living out Scripture's imperatives.

The sacraments as the "real presence" of Christ are the "nourishing and sustaining" presence of Christ that "invigorate and enliven our soul" and "nourish, refresh, strengthen and gladden."[6] The sacraments are given to us because of our feebleness, our need for something that will empower us to live out the commands of God faithfully.[7] For the believer seeking to live out faithfully the wisdom of the Spirit in obedient action, the Lord's Supper is "an exhortation than which no other could urge or animate us more strongly both to purity and holiness of life and also to charity, peace and concord."[8] The Word is empowered by the Spirit in the sacraments.

For most churches, this would be a radical, but not necessarily difficult, shift. To do so would mean that governing boards would have to train and authorize lay leaders to administer the Lord's Supper. It would also mean that the Supper itself would need to be practiced as a more regular part of the church life around more "ordinary" meals than the typical silver-utensiled ecclesiastical "high tea" that is now the case.

For some years now, I have led retreats or home gatherings where the Lord's Supper was actually celebrated as Jesus would have—as part of the meal itself. Blessings from the ancient church are used to lead the meal, songs are sung to give praise to God before and after. And amidst the dinner conversation and sharing of lives, bread is broken in remembrance of Jesus and passed to one another. As the Supper comes to an end, we fill a goblet with wine, give thanks, and remind one another that Jesus took a cup of wine and declared it the sign of the new covenant. With the encouragement to drink in remembrance of him, we drink together and then offer a prayer and sung doxology.

These "Dinner at the Lord's Table" meals are always deeply meaningful, expressly because they are so much like the practice of the early church, so much a part of our everyday life, so full of the extraordinary presence of God in the ordinary activity of the day. As Robert Banks has written, "[God's] extraordinariness is never so evident and powerful than when it expresses itself through the most ordinary event of relationship, experience or activity."[9]

Once it becomes obvious that the Word is to be performed and that the Lord's Supper should be the central sanctifying event of the trinitarian community, we are then inspired to other shared practices. Like Ezra who read the Word of God with a new "interpretation" in Nehemiah 8, resulting in a recovery of the Law, our "repentance" or turning to the Scriptures along trinitarian lines will lead to a recovery of practices for reading the Scriptures in a shared way. I want to suggest three explicitly communal practices:

- *Shared storytelling* for strengthening biblical literacy
- *Shared study* for strengthening biblical conversation
- *Shared meditation* for strengthening biblical praying

Shared Stories

First, in accordance with the conviction that the community of God is formed and nurtured by the stories of the Father's love, the church needs a concerted effort to strengthen biblical literacy through the teaching of the "shared narratives" of the Bible. Biblical literacy is necessary for the church to remain faithful to its own story. Writing about my own Presbyterian tradition, George Stroup identifies both the cause and effect of biblical illiteracy: "The 'people of the Book' no longer know what is in the Book, and the result is that Presbyterians do not understand why they live and worship in Reformed communities."[10]

If we are to live faithfully the stories of Jesus, we must know them. If we are going to discern the way of Jesus, we must be able to recognize the path that Jesus has trodden, the traveling habits, and the terrain covered in the story of redemption. If we are to be the community that lives according to our narrative and when necessary challenges tradition, then we must have the depth of understanding that comes from knowing not only individual verses, but whole sections of the Bible. We must understand the themes, the contradictions, the fabric of faithfulness and failure that make up the history of the people of God. We will never make sense of our struggles, suffering, and sin, our salvation, sanctification, and service, if we do not know the journey of our mothers and fathers in the faith. A people of the story must know, know deeply, and know by heart the story.

In my own congregation, we regularly preach, teach, and explore the practical dimensions of the central New Testament theme, "the kingdom of heaven." The five discourses of Matthew's Gospel have been preached, sermon series on living in and living out the kingdom of heaven that has come near in Jesus Christ are offered, visual arts depict the kingdom, and often displayed in the front of the chancel is a large banner that reminds people that the good news of Jesus was that "the Kingdom of heaven has come near" (Matt. 4:17). In order to teach the broad theme, "kingdom" language permeates our community life.

This narrative approach extends to our church's vision statement and church life. We repeatedly use themes and reinforce the notion that we are "the people of God" meant to bless the world. (Gen. 12:1; 1 Peter 2:9–10). Every year a month of sermons is set aside for teaching and preaching our vision statement that we are a "Community for the community." We have regular testimonies from church members in which they tell their story of how they came to find a "place to belong in the family of God, a place to grow in Jesus Christ, and a place to serve by the leading and the power of the Holy Spirit." Three times a year we offer a whole-church, multigenerational meal and worship service, called "Fifth Wednesday," where we eat together and then worship with a blend of styles representing everything from the kids' fun songs to praise choruses to one of the great hymns of the faith. The "sermon" for the evening is a faith-story by two or three people or by one family. At a recent gathering, a teenage girl, her mother, and her grandmother and grandfather all spoke—three generations telling the story of how God had transformed their family. From the teenager who had found that the church was the only place free from the negative attitudes of her school campus, to the mother and grandmother who have become church leaders, to the grandfather who didn't come to faith until the past year, in his seventies, that family shared their story as a living example of the biblical story of life transformation.

Shared Study

While biblical illiteracy cuts us off from our shared stories, our individualistic use of the Scriptures keeps us from the shared reality of Scripture working in us together. Because this is so, most of us don't realize that the transforming power of the Spirit works within each believer personally but not independently.

Richard Hays demonstrates that in the New Testament the community, not the individual Christian is the "primary addressee of God's imperatives."[11] The Bible is primarily focused not on teaching the individual person how to live in a God-honoring way, but on how the community can be a faithful witness to God together. Therefore, spiritual transformation always takes place, and spiritual experiences are always interpreted within the community as the distinctive place for forming believers.

> Shaped by the biblical narrative, the Community is where the story of salvation is experienced anew through the scripture, the Eucharist, prayers, hymns and other practices, as well as lived out in discipleship. Through our participation in Community, the biblical narrative forms and shapes our affections by providing descriptive access to the history, character and promises of God. Because our relationship with God is lived out within such a Community, *it does not only consist of some free-flowing set of experiences but is governed and shaped by the biblical narrative itself.*[12]

The Scriptures interpreted within the Spirit-led community are the only "authority"[13] by which we can "test" our spiritual experience and guide our discipleship. A transforming communion, therefore, is the community formed by, led by, and nourished by the Scriptures, within the sacramental shared life of the church.[14] That communion is only further enhanced if the community is all studying the same texts together.

While some traditions value the lectionary, and others reject it as too rigid and irrelevant to the changing demands of a community life,[15] I would suggest that even an informal, shared "lectionary" where a community covenants to read together the same texts would go a long way toward connecting it more closely to Christ and each other. Churches could develop Bible reading programs that are available to the entire congregation to read the same biblical texts together.[16] In our church, our small groups all study (to different degrees of depth, depending upon the maturity of the group) the same passage preached in worship. Regularly throughout the year, we produce devotional manuals and family prayer guides to coincide with the sermons, so that the whole community is learning together. Every week, whoever preaches the sermon also teaches a mid-week study of a more in-depth nature, and our church staff spends forty-five minutes every week studying the sermon passage together, so that we can better live out and lead our church into faithful performance of the text.

For at least one or two seasons a year, our child and youth curricula intentionally coincide with the adult materials so that families are learning (and parents are teaching!) together. And now we offer a "discuss the sermon in depth class" at each worship hour, led by a trained teacher.

Our intention is that every one of us who have heard the same Word of God proclaimed will have more opportunities throughout the week to dwell in the sermon text. Think about how much more deeply our lives would be changed if families and friends together were sharing, talking about, and encouraging one another to live out the same texts.

Last year, my son, Brooks, and I went on a father-son backpacking trip with some others from our church. One of the things the leaders asked us to do was for each father and son to go off for three hours together, to read, pray, and talk. They assigned us a task of coming up with a Bible verse that would be "ours" together and that we would use to remember this trip.

We talked about a number of verses (you can easily imagine that as both a pastor and a father I had more than a few ideas). But Brooks wanted us to memorize part of the psalm that we had read in worship the morning that we left for the trip. That Sunday morning, we arrived at our earliest service in our hiking clothes, and the call to worship on the overhead screens, from Psalm 95, talked about how the mountains belong to God.

And as we sat together that day on a mountainside, he said, "I want that to be our verse." So my son and I memorized a passage of Psalm 95 together. It is "our text" and a special bond between us. How much different would the Word transform us if the Bible were shared between us, in families, in homes, and in friendships.

Please don't misunderstand me. I'm not telling you that you shouldn't have individual times of reading the Bible. I'm just saying that when I have to open the Scripture with somebody else who asks me, "Well, Tod, are you living it?" I tend to do so more faithfully.

Through steps like these there is some recovery of a shared, communal learning of the Scriptures more characteristic in earlier centuries when the Scripture was mostly learned by hearing, in a common setting. While large churches with very diverse populations will be limited in the degree to which this can be implemented, some intentional effort to coordinate around key stories, themes, and concepts could still be fruitful.

For example, for ten years I served in the educational ministries department of a 4,000-member church in a diverse urban environment. Less than 25 percent of our congregation came from a Presbyterian background, and we were even more diverse economically and socially. Many of our adult education groups contained both homeless and near-homeless people and the highly educated and wealthy. Yet once a year we conducted an extended education series in which every adult class (fifteen in all), every small group (dozens), and the worship services all focused around the same biblical passages or creedal text. Though the vastly differing needs of people prohibited this approach all the time, this "unified curriculum" has borne some very positive results in shared learning and unified community themes.

Shared Meditation

Lastly, the "personal nature" of the Scriptures leads naturally to a prayerful response. To facilitate this, we need a recovery of what James McClendon refers to as "spiritual exegesis."[17] This involves shared meditation through communal reading of texts that are considered "direct address" from God calling for a personal response. "It is the readers who are the object as the God who is present in the Bible speaks through the Spirit. . . . By entering into the Biblical world, readers encounter the word of revelation for us."[18] This is experienced in many different forms where the Scripture is read contemplatively or imaginatively.[19]

One example is the *lectio divina* common to the Benedictine tradition. In this practice, the Scriptures are understood to be the very presence of God directly addressing the readers.[20] They are not read so much for information as for encounter, and the meditation takes place in a community where mutual accountability and correction coincide with personal direction. Covenant communities would wrestle with the texts together, confessing when they fail and returning together to the word of grace that bound them together in the first place.

In our church, every Advent and Lent, we offer a "contemplative service" every Friday morning from 7:00 to 8:00. In a quiet, candlelit room, with soft music playing, people are invited to read a common text (usually the text for the sermon that week) and pray silently for thirty minutes. Then the leader brings the group together for thirty minutes of liturgy and *lectio divina*. This prayerful time around the Scriptures has been deeply meaningful even for busy people who have to rearrange their lives to fit in an hour of morning prayer. Certainly every person can do it alone, but the power of praying the Scriptures together—even silently—is unmistakable.

The result of these practices is recovery of a shared spiritual life: shared stories (narratives), shared study (biblical lectionary of exposition and devotion), and shared meditation (spiritual exegesis). As the stories of the community are told around a table, connecting the proclaimed Word to the gift of God in the sacraments, grace and command, power and instruction are inextricably tied together. The community remembers the past saving acts of God ("'Do this in remembrance of me'"—1 Cor. 11:24), participates in the present saving activity of God ("The bread we break, is it not a sharing in the body of Christ?"—1 Cor. 10:16), and proclaims the saving acts of God until the future consummation ("proclaim the Lord's death until he comes"—1 Cor. 11:26). In the community of Word as Scripture and sacrament, the perichoretic presence of God in story, icon, and wisdom transforms the life of the believer and the shared life of the church.

The Word That Transforms

Leonid Ouspensky wrote: "It is the nature of holiness to sanctify that which surrounds it."[21] The "word that transforms" us is the holy Word that surrounds us in the divine embrace and sanctifies us. The trinitarian love that extends into the world in the Word, Jesus Christ encounters us now in the Word as Scripture and sacrament. When the community of Christ comes together as a living embodiment of and participation in that Trinity, we gather around a table with a loaf and a cup and an open book. This gathering shows us Christ, tells us our story, and serves as a lamp to our future steps. In it the Word is present, the living and active Word that brought the Earth into being, parted the Red Sea, instructed through the Law and corrected through the prophets, became flesh and walked and lived and prayed and cried out from a cross, was poured out at Pentecost, and lives in each gathering of believers as the icon of the grace of Christ, the story of the divine love of the Father and the wisdom of the Spirit. This Word transforms us.

10

Transforming Witness I

Praying with Jesus

In the movie *For Love of the Game,* an aging baseball player named Billy Chapel is pitching in Yankee Stadium in what could be the last game of his career. Through flashbacks we see the events that led up to this moment. Jane, his on-again-off-again girlfriend, has broken off with him, punctuating her feelings by saying, "You don't need me. You and the ball and the diamond, you're perfect. . . . You can win or lose the game all by yourself." And she left him.

While the flashbacks tell us of his inner turmoil, in the middle of the baseball diamond Billy Chapel is pitching a perfect game. A perfect game is the rarest feat in sports. It is a game in which a pitcher records twenty-seven consecutive outs. Three batters each inning, three outs, nine innings. No one reaches base. Not one hit, not one walk, not one error. Perfect.

Even though he is forty years old, Billy Chapel starts off the game strong, striking out batters. But as he comes in to start the eighth inning, he says to his catcher, "I don't know if I have anything left." His catcher looks at him and says, "Chappy, you just throw whatever you got, whatever's left. The boys are all here for you, we'll back you up, we'll be there. . . . We're gonna be awesome for you right now. Just throw."

As he starts the inning he throws three straight balls. One more, and he'll walk the batter, ruining his perfect game. In his mind's eye he sees his father reminding him to be calm. He pitches a strike, and then the next ball is hit so hard it looks like a game-wrecking home run—only to be stolen away as one of the outfielders makes a spectacular leaping catch. The catcher is right. The boys are there for him. It takes the heroic defensive plays of his fielders behind him, of his teammates, to ultimately save the game for him: an unlikely grab by the catcher, a long throw from third, a diving stop at short. He even adds a prayer. A remarkable win: he gets the perfect game.

But Jane's words haunt him, "You don't need me . . . you can win or lose the game all by yourself." At that moment, he realizes that he is not perfect alone. He needs the help of his teammates, he needs the memory of his father, he needs Jane's love, he even needs a little divine intervention. No one is perfect alone.

Ministry is like baseball. To follow Christ and serve others requires a great deal of individual effort, but we cannot do it alone. In a wonderful, mysterious way, even the Trinity teaches us that.

We've noted that the center of focus in Rublev's icon of the Holy Trinity is not the divine figures, but the chalice of wine. It sits in the center as a single shared cup, bidding us to come, partake, and—in doing so—share in the fellowship and redemptive activity of God. While we celebrate the community of shared love that exists in the Godhead and is expressed in the fellowship of the church, the true center of the divine communion is the shared sacrificial love offered to the world. For when it is poured out, it reveals the true character of that communion for which our souls are restless, to which we are invited, and in which life is found.

The chalice in the center is a reminder that we are called to the fellowship of a relationship with God, but that intimacy with God cannot be separated from the work of God. You and I are invited to the fellowship, but with the invitation comes the call to carry out the work.

For many of us, there is a concern that an emphasis on community will take away from the Great Commission (Matt. 28:19–20). We all know too many Christian groups that become nothing more than holy cliques, insular and self-absorbed Christian country clubs more concerned about securing good parking for their members than extending themselves to others. What about evangelism and ministry? some of us may ask. Isn't the church really about sharing the faith, sending out missionaries and preaching the gospel? Isn't the church really about being a witness? Yes. The community's very raison d'être is to witness to the presence of the triune communion, and, staying consistent with the theme of this book, to do so in a manner that reflects that triune communion.

Indeed, the last words Jesus said to his disciples before his ascension into heaven was that once the Holy Spirit came upon them, they would be his "witnesses in Jerusalem, in all Judea and Samaria, and to the ends of the earth" (Acts 1:8). This has, of course, been the purpose for God's people from the calling of the first follower. In Genesis 12:1–3, the election of Abram demonstrates that God's gracious election of a people is both a *relationship* with God and a *role* in God's redemptive activity: *"I will bless you . . . so that you will be a blessing. . . . and in you all the families of the earth shall be blessed."*

Because this is so, to be God's people is to participate in both fellowship with God and the ministry of God. But to be sure, in the same way that the call of one man (Abram) led to the calling of a nation, the call of Jesus to be the savior of the world, leads to his people being a community of witness to that saving love in the world. In short, our community is not only *for* witness, it *is* witness.

In Acts 2 we read of the early church. Just days after Jesus told his disciples that they'd be his witnesses, the Holy Spirit is poured out upon the small band of followers, the gospel is proclaimed, and 3,000 are saved and baptized. Then in verses 46 and 47 we read:

> Day by day, as they spent much time together in the temple, they broke bread at home and ate their food with glad and generous hearts, praising God and having the goodwill of all the people. And day by day the Lord added to their number those who were being saved.

In the earliest church, we have the earliest model for witness. Even before they were "sent" throughout the Roman Empire, the new followers were surprisingly effective evangelists simply by being together. Richard Hays says, "The community, in its corporate life, is called to embody *an alternative order that stands as a sign of God's redemptive purposes in the world.*"[1]

The church's corporate life—its shared life—is a participation in the Communion of God and a witness to the loving presence of God in the world. Indeed, we now see not only *how* God transforms lives, but *why*. The Triune God's intention is to reveal himself to the world. And our ministry is our participation in that divine intention. To reveal God is to glorify God. To glorify God is to reveal God as God truly is—as Father, Son, and Holy Spirit, the God who is love and who is lovingly involved in the world.

Love and Glory

Love, to be love, must be expressed. It is impossible to claim love while not acting in a loving way (1 John 3:17–18). If God is love and the essence of God is loving relationship, the very nature of God's being is one of extending the love of God to others. In the same way, if the essence of the church is the love of God expressed among Christians, then the very nature of the church will necessarily be to extend the love experienced in that fellowship to others.

After five years of dating and five years of marriage, my wife Beth and I had finally come to the place where, secure in our love for each other, we had an overflow of love that we could offer a child. When our marriage was immature, we were scared about having a baby. But the stronger our marriage became, the more we wanted to share the love we experienced with someone new.

In the same way, I have never known a Christian who was growing in faith, secure in a fellowship, profoundly aware of the grace of God, and empowered by the Spirit, who did not want to extend himself or herself graciously to other people. Whenever I see churches that don't want to reach out to others in evangelism and mission, or see Christians who don't want to share their faith or welcome unbelievers to their churches, it is usually because there is brokenness in the middle of the community. Pastors can harangue about the eternal importance of saving souls, but if people feel disconnected, disregarded, or discouraged, they will not extend themselves to others. When hurt abounds, ministry flounders. But when love is ample, ministry flourishes.

The Transforming Witness

The transforming communion of the church is meant to be the place where we genuinely experience and sincerely extend the love of the Trinity. By our lives and with our lips we witness to that which we have experienced and invite others to partake; we bear witness to how our lives have been transformed and offer that same life-transforming power to others. The "transforming witness" is the church proclaiming and demonstrating the present reality of the love of the Triune God by its participation in the redemptive activities of God. It begins in prayer, depends upon discernment, and is expressed in ministry. And to be truly exceptional, it is all done as a community—together.

First, we will examine prayer as the church's participation in the intercession of Jesus by being a "communion of sanctification." Second, we will learn that discernment is a communal exercise for the edification of the Spirit that develops wisdom for the community's witness. And lastly, we will look at ministry as revealing or glorifying the Triune God lovingly at work in the world. Along the way, it will become clear that in every aspect of ministry there is both the transformation of the minister and the witness to God who is transforming and working through each ministering person. In short, as the church is sanctified in transforming communion—beginning in prayer, depending on discernment, and expressed in ministry—it serves as a witness to God's gracious invitation and suffering love present in the world.

Prayer and the Communion of Sanctification

In C. S. Lewis's *The Screwtape Letters,* the senior devil Screwtape writes to his nefarious apprentice, Wormwood, about how to manipulate a young Christian's prayer life so that it will actually work against his growing in faith. If Wormwood is going to tempt the Christian into a feeble and meaningless faith, then when he prays, writes Screwtape, "You must bring him to a condition in which he can practice self-examination for an hour without discovering any of those facts about himself which are perfectly clear to anyone who has even lived in the same house with him or worked in the same office." Further, when discussing the Christian's prayers for his mother (by whom he is mildly annoyed and from whom obviously estranged), Screwtape writes, "It is no doubt impossible to prevent his praying for his mother, but we have means of rendering the prayers innocuous. Make sure that they are always very 'spiritual,' that he is always concerned with the state of her soul and never with her rheumatism."[2]

In biting prose, Lewis's Screwtape points to two deeply problematic areas in most prayers. Our prayers don't change us, and they don't truly engage the real problems of real people. Functioning as a kind of spiritual denial, prayers when kept in the privacy of one's inner life only reinforce our isolation from the transforming love that comes through the community. I don't think there could be a better description of the exact opposite intention of Jesus' prayers. But of course, that is what a demon would encourage, isn't it?

The "transforming witness" begins in participating in Jesus' own shared prayer for his own sanctification as we hear it in John 17.[3] While space does not afford us a full examination of that prayer here,[4] one section does help us to see how Jesus prayed and intended his followers to pray as they sought to be witnesses to God in the world.

In John 17, Jesus prays that his purposes in life, death, and resurrection "may be perfectly fulfilled through what he now does and through his followers."[5] This purpose is fulfilled through the sanctification of Jesus and the disciples, for which Jesus intercedes with the Father.[6]

> I am not asking you to take them out of the world, but I ask you to protect them from the evil one. . . . Sanctify them in the truth; your word is truth. As you have sent me into the world, so I have sent them into the world. And for their sakes I sanctify myself, so that they also may be sanctified in truth. . . . "I ask not only on behalf of these, but also on behalf of those who will believe in me through their word, that they may all be one. As you, Father, are in me and I am in you, may they also be in us, so that the world may believe that you have sent me. The glory that you have given me I have given them, so that they may be one, as we are one, I in them and you in me, that they may

> become completely one, so that the world may know that you have sent me and have loved them even as you have loved me.

In this prayer, we see Jesus praying on behalf of himself, his followers, and all future disciples (v. 20). His prayer consists of three requests:

1. that his followers would be in the world like he has been in the world, both protected and sent (vv. 15, 18)
2. that his followers would be sanctified the way he has been sanctified for the sake of the world (vv. 17, 19)
3. that his followers would be as unified with each other as he has been with the Father for the sake of the world (vv. 21–23).[7]

Notice what he doesn't pray. He doesn't pray, "Oh, God, keep them healthy and successful. Give them what they want, and make them happy." His prayer is "God, as you continue to work in me as I complete my work in the world, keep my disciples in the world and move within them. Change them, sanctify them. Make them holy in the truth of your word." What does Jesus pray for us? That we would be in the world as his representative, with his character, fulfilling and completing his mission.

What is most significant is the centrality of the whole notion of "sanctification" in this prayer. This is a prayer in which Jesus is asking God to set him apart and, by extension, set his followers apart from the world, so that they can live for the world. The sanctification of Jesus leads to the sanctification of Jesus' disciples.[8] As Jesus dedicates himself to the fulfillment of his purposes, the disciples are given the charge to continue the work that Jesus had begun—the ministry of glorifying or revealing God—through their own transformation (John 17:20–23).[9]

In John 17, we have both a public prayer that reveals the purposes of the Trinity and a personal instruction[10] that guides us in our witness: all witness begins in being prayerfully sanctified by God and in being prayerfully unified with each other. Through prayer we are made holy, bound together, and enabled to serve as witnesses to the transforming love of God.

In this, we see Jesus' own prayer as a statement of trinitarian purpose and process.[11] Prayer, when practiced as part of a God-revealing community, is a discipline of both truth and loyalty. It binds disciples to Jesus and protects them from error that would bring division and lead them astray. It conforms the community to the character of God revealed in Jesus Christ's mission to the world. In verses 17–19 we read,

> Sanctify them in the truth; your word is truth. As you have sent me into the world, so I have sent them into the world. And for their sakes I sanctify myself, so that they also may be sanctified in truth.

We then see that as the disciples are loyal to the truth of the revelation of God in Jesus, are unified as a reflection of Jesus' relationship to the Father, and participate in God's loving self-revelation in the world, they are "sanctified" as participants in the Trinity and "witness to God."

> In the prayer the basis of the unity of the Church is the nature of God and the reality of his redemptive activity. More specifically, it is an outflow of the relations within the Triune God and of his action in and through the incarnate Son, whereby his saving sovereignty became operative in the world.[12]

The prayerful community that reaches into the world as the witness for Christ is one that is being transformed through the truth of Jesus and unity with other believers in holiness for the sake of the world. Christ is center, our love for each other holds us together, we are changed and glorify or witness to God's life-changing power in the world.

From Jesus' Prayer to Our Praying

We can't overlook the fact that this instruction is given in the form of a prayer. Jesus doesn't so much exhort his disciples to truth, unity, and faithfulness as he asks God to so work in them that they would, as participants in his ministry, experience the same power operative in him. In the same way as Jesus prays for the church, so the church must also be faithful in prayer, so that all ministry is an expression of God's power lovingly at work in the world.[13] Indeed, carrying on the priestly ministry of Jesus' intercession is no less a part of the ministry of the body of Christ than is extending the love of Jesus. Through persistent prayerful intercession, the body of Christ continues to receive the power of God that "keeps" and "sanctifies" the church and grounds its work in the work of God.

But how, practically, can the church fulfill both the charge in the prayer and the model of being prayerful? What steps toward encouraging communal participation in the ministry of intercession will empower it and encourage loyalty to the truth, unity, and participation in the suffering love ministry of Jesus? Let me suggest one tangible step that will foster participation in the communion of sanctification: reconfiguring church leadership (both lay and clergy) as a missional "order" for serving the church through example, instruction, and intercession.[14]

Church leadership as a missional "order"

> There is nothing so contagious as holiness, nothing more pervasive than prayer. This is precisely what the traditional Church means by evangelism and what distinguishes it from recruitment.
>
> Martin Thornton[15]

While John 17 is traditionally regarded as Jesus' "high priestly prayer" and offered as an example of Jesus' intercessory ministry "at the right hand of the Father," the setting of the prayer is within the context of the earthly ministry of Jesus.[16] As such, the prayer is an example of the priestly ministry to which all believers are called and a model of faithfulness and intercession that leads to all being "sanctified." Indeed, following the model of Jesus, the whole church should engage in the "priestly ministry" of personal faithfulness, instruction, and intercession.

However, some have pointed out that the Reformers' emphasis on the "priesthood of all believers" has had an unfortunate side effect. "Theoretically, it should uplift all believers, but in actual fact it tends to reduce them to the lowest common denominator. We wanted to make everyone in church into robust saints but succeeded only in making mostly mediocre ones."[17]

Recently, a resurgence of neo-Anabaptist ecclesiology has offered a similar critique.[18] Yet, as Chan warns, "the Anabaptist model of the voluntary church that restricted membership to committed individuals offered one solution. But a small church of pure souls is at best a short-term solution. It will either become an exclusive club or won't be pure for long once it starts mass evangelization."[19] Chan suggests an alternative based upon Anglo-catholic writer Martin Thornton's idea of a "remnant."[20] Thornton envisions the remnant as a body of people within a larger "visible community" that is committed to a corporate "rule" and prayer for the sake of igniting renewal.[21]

While I find Thornton's "remnant" language biblically imprecise,[22] he points the way to a reconfiguring of church leadership for the purpose of spiritual renewal and witness, and not merely for administrative efficiency or the pastoral care of the saints. In our church in San Clemente, corporate prayer has been the single most difficult discipline to institute. While many individuals are committed to praying privately, being part of prayer chains or leading in prayer during a worship service, joint prayer gatherings are ill-attended unless there is a critical need.

On September 11, 2001, hundreds showed up to pray; when a dear saint in the church has cancer, we get dozens; when we are looking for a desperately needed associate pastor, we get a good-sized group; but when we gather to pray regularly for the mission of our church in the world, only a small and faithful "remnant" shows up. After many discussions, we've decided that this corporate work of intercession will depend on the church leaders who commit to come together once a month. We invite the whole church, but generally only the leaders show up. While this is sometimes discouraging to us, there is still a sense that our job as elders and pastors includes praying together for the church. It is now a primary shared responsibility we embrace.

The transforming witness that begins in prayer in the life of a faith community begins with leaders recasting their primary responsibilities for embodying discipleship as an alternative way of life and seeking to revitalize the larger community through their example and prayer. These leaders, both lay and clergy, would follow the example of the Twelve in Acts 6, who are focused upon prayer and the Word and would offer leadership by example, instruction, and intercession. Following the model of Jesus, missional leaders would "sanctify themselves" by their faithful actions and would pray for the sanctifying of others as God sovereignly moves in each person's life.[23] While they certainly would have different tasks to perform in service of the church, their primary call would be to lead the community in its witness to the greater world. While pastors would give leadership, and would continue preaching for the larger church, they would also increasingly serve as "equippers" and spiritual directors for the ministry and maturity of the missional leaders (Eph. 4:1–13).

I envision a day when spiritual leaders will still take on church "committee" roles as an expression of their work in the community (like someone in a monastic order would have a different community task) but will sense their primary "call" is to make disciples through a ministry of the Word and prayer. Increasingly, even larger churches are letting small sessions and boards function as ministry management teams while giving over to well-mobilized and well-equipped lay leaders more ministries and mission work. Certainly, many of the tasks of church life don't require great spiritual maturity, just a willing spirit.

Darrell Guder and his colleagues call this "order of spiritual ardor" a "covenant community" within the larger congregation, that is, "a bounded set comprised of those who have chosen to take on the commitment practices and disciplines that make them a distinct missionary community."[24] These mutually agreed-upon commitment practices and disciplines would make up a kind of shared "rule" for spiritual growth to be practiced by the leadership as a faithful example and on behalf of the community.[25] As the missional leaders share the fellowship of the covenant community, keep the rule and serve as intercessors for the larger church, they will fulfill the intentions of Jesus' prayer in John 17. The spiritual disciplines centered in Scripture reading and study would help to "keep them in [God's] name" and "sanctify them in the truth"; the fellowship and shared "rule" would demonstrate a unity that is focused on love for one another, faithfulness to Christ, and their ministry of intercessory prayer.

Significantly, the traditional location of John 17 is Jesus' last supper with his disciples.[26] Preparing for his death, Jesus gives his disciples an example of how they should live with one another by serving them, giving them the meal, instructing them, and praying for them. As Jesus gives the meal to his disciples as a "remembrance" of him, he is instructing them on the most important "spiritual discipline" of the transforming communion and the most regular expression of their common life. For Paul, this meal would become "the central action by which the community maintains and deepens its life"[27] and a "proclamation" to both the community and the world of the "Lord's death until he comes."[28] If, as Beasley-Murray suggests, the language of John 17:19 is meant to call to mind the communion language of the bread and cup "on behalf of many," then we need to emphasize the Lord's Supper as not only an act of fellowship with believers,[29] but also instruction to the covenant community on how to live "on behalf of others" according to the manner of Jesus.[30]

The ultimate concern of the meal, then, is not (as is so often discussed) who administers, the precise understanding of Jesus' "presence," or the wording used, but instead the divine calling of the fellowship to holy character and loving concern for one another.[31] The ethical dimension of the meal as described in Paul's correction in 1 Corinthians 11:17–34 is one of laying aside personal fulfillment (even "spiritual" fulfillment) and "waiting for one another." Thus, in sharing the meal according to the manner of Jesus, each disciple not only participates in the proclamation of Jesus' death through the meal, but also is instructed in the proper attitude for relating to other believers and entering into the world.

In my church we spent a good season of time having the session board of the church meet several times a year for training and for enjoying a meal where the Lord's Supper was celebrated. In these meals and through the instruction, the leadership learned that our prayerful ministry was always to be a shared commemoration of Jesus' own sacrificial love for the world.

I envision a day when this covenant community of leaders would themselves lead similar gatherings throughout our larger church in homes in every neighborhood. The ministry of this covenant community would be to lead our church to be a community for the world. Jesus' intercession and instruction leads to the covenant community's intercession and instruction, which then leads to the church's intercession and witness to the world.

Through the instruction given in the meal and the example of Jesus' own intercession, we have a model for the church to grow as a sanctifying communion. The body of Christ is to be the answer to Jesus' prayer in John 17. Like Jesus, the church "sanctifies itself" and prays for the sanctification of the world by God's gracious intervention.[32] Like Jesus, the church prays to fulfill its call to live "on behalf of others," to be faithful to the Father, and to proclaim the reality of God's kingdom come near (Mark 1:14–15) and made available to all as "newness of life" in Jesus' death (Rom. 6:3–4). But the specific actions of witness require more than just prayer; they require faithfulness of action. So what begins in prayer depends on discernment, which is the subject of our next chapter.

11

Transforming Witness II

Discernment and Wisdom

In recent decades, discerning the will of God has become a contentious and often poorly handled matter. Just consider these vignettes, all from my own experience.

An elder in my church came up to me right before I made a presentation to the congregation of an $8 million building project and said to me, "Pastor, I will vote for this project because I believe that if you have prayed about it and God told you to do this, then we should do it. I trust that you can discern God's will."

A presbytery executive told our search committee when they were looking for an associate pastor that their job was to "search for the person that God has already picked out for you. There is one person out there that God wants to be an associate pastor in this church, and your job is to discern God's will."

A frustrated friend who serves as an elder at his church said, "Every time our pastor gets a new hare-brained idea, he says that God told him that this was his will for our church, and then none of us dare dispute him. It's like he is the only one who can discern God's will."

The notion of discerning and doing God's will is considered by most to be a requirement for Christian living and even more so for

Christian ministry. But there is not one place in the New Testament where Christians "discern God's will." That is not to say that discernment and the will of God are not important, it's just that they are often confused.

While our transforming witness begins in prayer as participation in Jesus' sanctifying ministry, it depends upon discernment. More specifically, witness depends upon the edification of the Spirit that comes through discernment. Indeed, in the New Testament the act of discernment is one of the primary modes of personal transformation. While prayer is the source of transformation, discernment is the instrument.

When one approaches the subject of discernment, there is no shortage of resources offering help. Throughout the centuries, individual Christians have sought to determine how to respond faithfully to God in personal life situations.[1] However, at this point we must pause. As I said before, most people tend to confuse discernment with personal wisdom and guidance; that discernment is about how to make individual decisions. But a review of the biblical understanding of discernment reveals that it is principally part of the moral life of the community of God's people, expressly for the edification of the church.[2] Indeed, the key question of being a witness in the world is a discernment question for the community together: "Based upon who you are as that is revealed in what you are doing, O God, among us and within us, who should we be and what should we do in response?"[3]

What Does the Bible Really Say?

> Do not be conformed to this world, but be transformed by the renewing of your minds, so that you may *discern* what is the will of God—what is good and acceptable and perfect.
>
> Romans 12:2

> Do not despise the words of prophets, but *test everything*; hold fast to what is good; abstain from every form of evil.
>
> 1 Thessalonians 5:20–22

> *Try to find out* what is pleasing to the Lord. Take no part in the unfruitful works of darkness, but instead expose them.
>
> Ephesians 5:10–11

> And this is my prayer, that your love may overflow more and more with knowledge and full insight to *help you to determine* what is best, so that in the day of Christ you may be pure and blameless, having produced the harvest of righteousness that comes through Jesus Christ for the glory and praise of God.
>
> Philippians 1:9–11

> Examine yourselves to see whether you are living in the faith. *Test yourselves*. Do you not realize that Jesus Christ is in you?—unless, indeed, you fail to meet the test!
>
> 2 Corinthians 13:5

These passages (in which I have added emphasis to highlight similar key terms) demonstrate that the overriding aim of discernment is the moral dimension. In every case, the issue at hand is not a method of "spiritual decision-making,"[4] but discerning good and evil at work within the community of faith.[5] It is a corporate, and not merely individualistic, process whereby the Christian community grows in faithfulness and holiness.[6] The end result of the discernment or "testing" is to "hold fast to what is good; abstain from every form of evil;" to "take no part in the unfruitful works of darkness, but instead expose them," "so that in the day of Christ you may be pure and blameless" (1 Thess. 5:21; Eph. 5:11; Phil. 1:10).

From this, it becomes apparent that discernment is not primarily that we decide personally and rightly, but that we decide communally and righteously.[7] From this we can conclude that according to the pattern of the New Testament, discernment is a moral communal process and discipline—which in turn leads to building up the body of Christ (i.e., the Christian community) in holiness. Through discernment and the holiness it produces, the prayerful community is equipped to live obediently and is transformed more and more into a distinguishable witness to the world.[8]

It's about Wisdom

Even if discernment is not, as it usually presupposed, a method of determining God's will in specific cases, but instead a means of distinguishing between good and evil and edifying the community, a process of some kind is still necessary. Throughout the New Testament when the community is devoted to prayer, nurtured in apostolic teaching, and open to the Spirit's manifestation through trusted people,[9] its moral discernment leads to wisdom. In the Bible, wisdom is less about a particular decision than an overall disposition of life built through many communal and moral decisions. And from the first century the Christian grid for making such decisions involved two criteria applied with equal commitment: the Word and the community—our obligation to obey God and to build up one another. You can't separate one from the other or pit one against the other. Wise decisions demand both. So, when Christians make a choice, they need to ask two questions:

1. *Is it consistent with the Word of God?* Is it consistent with the apostolic confession and instruction? Is it consistent with the principle of *sola scriptura,* the norm of the Christian life?[10]

2. *Does it build up, edify, and contribute to the well-being of the community of God's people?* Does it lead to the edification of the body of Christ for the purpose of holiness? Does it develop the church into a "community of character"?[11]

While most Christians will be quick to agree with the first principle, true discernment in both life and ministry requires another, much more neglected, step. If we want to make really blessed decisions, then we must not only listen to the word of Scripture, but also consider the impact on the community. In other words, in every decision, we should ask more than "Is this right for me?" We should also ask, "Is this right for us? How will this affect us? Will this decision make a negative impact on the church?" Even better, "Will it contribute to the well-being of my brothers and sisters in Christ?"

Frankly, we don't want to consider how our decisions affect others. And we certainly don't want others' opinions, advice, or counsel. We want to trust our own minds, our own hearts, our own insight. We want to solve our own problems and take care of our own dilemmas. We want to minister on our own steam and with our own agenda. Proverbs 12:15 says, "Fools think their own way is right, but the wise listen to advice." One of the single best ways to contribute to the well-being of the community and to make wise choices is to let the community weigh in on your choices.

When I was seeking ordination in the Presbyterian Church, I had to submit to a three-year process for clarifying my sense of call. Not only did I have educational, ministry, and examination requirements to fulfill, but I had to meet once a year with a committee of people who worked with me to determine my suitability for ordained ministry. They ensured that my life and character were consistent with biblical standards for ministers and that my giftedness was a good match for my aspirations. By the time the process was over, I had to be approved by three different church governing bodies: my home church that sent me, the presbytery that shepherded me, and finally, a church that was willing to call me as their pastor. While many people tend to describe "calling" as a private spiritual experience, in our denomination a pastor is not called until all three "communities" (the one sending, the one shepherding, and the one calling) confirm the call. It is from start to finish an act of the community.

Discernment is, then, the act of the people of God figuring out together whether a prophetic utterance, teaching, or decision is right or wrong, moral or immoral, the leading of the Spirit or of the flesh. This activity of discernment builds the body of Christ, which then produces wisdom for the rest of the decisions we have to make. The goal of discernment in the Scriptures is not figuring out the "will of God"; it is fulfilling the will of God in 1 Thessalonians 4:3: "your sanctification." What churches need is to practice moral discernment in order to become the kind of community that continually develops "spiritual poise"[12] for making everyday decisions according to the Scriptures that build up the whole body.

In an early Christian text called the Didache, the community is given instruction for evaluating a new prophet or itinerant preacher. First the teacher's message must be evaluated by whether it conforms to the "apostolic message" preached and passed on by the church. But that is not all. If a prophet stays more than two days without working, asks for money, or teaches falsely, then his words are to be ignored. If, on the other hand, he depends on the hospitality of the community for only a day or two, asks only for enough bread to make it to the next town, or willingly stays and works, then—if the messages prove consistent with the apostolic instruction—the prophet is to be welcomed, and the community is charged with caring for his needs.[13]

This pattern of discernment is biblical and communal, deeply personal and life-transforming. It reminds us that all true ministry comes from the Spirit's work in a community to form believers together into a community of witness.

Without prayer and discernment, ministry is not witness. Prayer anchors all ministry in the purposes of the Father; discernment assures that all ministry transforms the believer by the power of the Spirit, according to the likeness of the Son. Prayer and discernment together ensure that the ministry received and undertaken is an expression and embodiment of the Trinity—that is, that it glorifies God.

12

Transforming Witness III

Ministry and Glory

During a recent sermon, I stepped away from the lectern and left behind my notes. I instead scanned the congregation until I spotted Betsy. I said to everyone gathered, "Have all of you met Betsy? Betsy, do me a favor, will you? Please stand up." Then I went on to tell the whole congregation about Betsy's service in our church and our community. Betsy is a former youth missionary who now works for a charitable foundation giving away large sums of money to worthy causes. She is a mentor to young women in the foster-care system and is a small-group leader in our church. I ended this brief resume of her character by saying, "Would all of you please express how great it is to have Betsy in our church?" And five hundred people all applauded. I led that little tribute not only to highlight a remarkable person but also to illustrate a point. Biblically speaking, I "glorified" Betsy.

The term *to glorify* means "to shed light upon" or "to reveal." It is to focus the attention of others on the character and attributes of someone so that they will be seen as they are. To glorify God is then to reveal God as God is—the Triune God whose essence is love and who is present and active in the world by participating in God's own activities of revelation and reconciliation (Eph. 1:8b–12). If ministry is glorifying or revealing God as God is, then it is also revealing the God who is already ministering in the world.[1] To glorify God is to proclaim and demonstrate the good news of God's reign and rule already available in Jesus (Matt. 28:19–20), to gather people as disciples in communion with God (Matt. 23:37; Eph. 1:9–10) as an adopted people of God (Rom. 8:14–16; Gal. 4:4–7; Eph. 1:5) who worship God (Isa. 55:11; Luke 10:17–18; John 20:31; 2 Peter 3:9; Rev. 4–5) and are transformed into his image in Christ (Rom. 8:29–30), living to the praise of God's glory (Eph. 1:12) *in the world* (1 Peter 2:12). In short, to glorify God is to make the divine table fellowship of the Triune God visible in the world through our participation in it.

Let's return to that chalice of wine sitting in the center of the table in Rublev's icon of the Holy Trinity. That chalice, symbolizing the poured-out blood of Christ, the sacrificial ministry to people, is the true focus. I believe that that chalice is meant to remind us that the center of any truly transforming communion is not the communion itself, but the sacrificial love that results from it. That is the true character of that Communion of God for which we our souls are restless, to which we are invited, and in which life is found. That is ministry: *It is the life of the community that is itself transformed by God and participates in God's own ministry of loving and saving the world.*

My friends, the community *is* the witness. The community that pours itself out together to a needy world, the church when it lives out its calling as a true transforming communion, is the most effective witness to the presence of God in the world.

But are there some specific activities that the community can do in order to be a more intentional and effective witness? Yes. Ministry that reveals the presence of the Triune God-Who-Is-Love in the world shares and bears the divine love of God for and to the world, reveals the presence of God's Spirit in the world, and includes every person in the fellowship of the Son for the transformation of the world. Or, to put it another way, the community is called together to be:

1. Bearers of divine love
2. Docents of the Spirit
3. Hosts at every table

All at the same time.

Bearers of Divine Love

> Because the inner love of the triune God is so great and overflowing, the Father chose to create a world which would be peopled by a race created in the image of his Son, so they could reflect the glory of the Son and share in the eternal life and blessedness of the Trinity.[2]

As "bearers" of divine love, our primary ministry is to proclaim and demonstrate the "great and overflowing" love of God to everyone: first to the community of believers and then to the world. As Jacques Ellul reminds us, to be a prayerful community is to be a witnessing community. "Total involvement in prayer demands of us a participation in society, in the lives of those close to us, of those at a distance, of intimate friends, and of strangers. Prayer has no limits."[3] To participate in prayer is to put oneself before God as the answer to the prayer. To pray for God to work in our families, our churches, or our worlds is to make oneself available for being God's instrument of love, first in the community of believers and then to the world.

In the Bible, ministry begins with expressing the love of God to the family of believers. This is so elemental that 1 John tells us to assume that if someone *does not show love* to Christian brothers and sisters, then we are safe to assume that they *do not know God* at all (1 John 4:7–11). In the Gospel of John, our love for believers is the sign to *unbelievers* that we are, in fact, Christ's disciples (John 13:35). And perhaps, most significant, the love that we show to other believers is a proclamation of the very presence of God in the world (John 17:21; cf. John 16:5–15).

But that shared love within the church does not simply stay in the church. We are bearers of the divine love to the world as a demonstration of God's initiating love for us "while we still were sinners" (1 John 4:10; Rom. 5:8). Our ministries through the church should incarnate that same love, especially to those who are not part of a congregation and therefore never hear the message.

In his book *The Church of Irresistible Influence,* pastor Robert Lewis describes how his congregation has intentionally moved into the world, building bridges of love for the message of the gospel to travel. In our San Clemente church we started the Jabez Community Outreach Ministry. Named after the popular book *The Prayer of Jabez,* by Bruce Wilkinson, this is an entirely lay-led ministry that is dedicated to expanding the influence of God's love by working with our local community organizations and supplying them with the resources of people and funds to carry out their charitable missions. As a church we decided that if another organization in town was doing good works in the community, then we wouldn't compete with them but would instead support them by bringing the tangible love of God to them. In just two short years, this burgeoning ministry has contributed thousands of dollars and deployed dozens of "our" people to serve in the local Boys and Girls Club, Family Assistance Ministry, a domestic-violence shelter, a low-income public school, and a Christian foster-care ministry. In addition, every time the city of San Clemente wants to host a positive gathering for the larger community, we lend support with volunteers and money. We support local sports leagues, we give to the city's Fourth of July fireworks show, we sponsor civic organizations' special events. Our health ministry and parish nurse program offers all of our ministries to the larger community. We began "Operation Home" to care for U. S. Marine families at nearby Camp Pendleton when the military personnel are deployed oversees. Our vision is to make our remodeled church campus a "spiritual community center" that gathers people together and welcomes our neighbors in God's love. Anything we can do to tangibly proclaim the love of God in our community, we do.

But it is not enough to bring the love of God to people; we must also help them recognize that God is already at work in the world—which leads to our second communal ministry.

Docents of the Spirit

A docent is a trained person who usually works in a museum pointing out works of art or other exhibits to the untutored eye. Without a docent most of us would not be able to even "see" much of what is before us. In a world filled with so many eager spiritual seekers, there is sadly little spiritual sight. So many who are busy looking for God miss the most obvious signs of God's presence at work in the world.

When Beth and I traveled to Paris some years ago, we made a visit to the Louvre. Since my wife was an art major in college, I had my own docent, who opened my eyes to the overwhelmingly magnificent works of art that filled room after room. Without her, I probably would have been lost. Like most people with minimal artistic awareness, I went into the Louvre mostly looking for the Mona Lisa. Indeed, I saw busloads of tourists stream past one masterpiece after another, all looking for this one specific work. Once they craned their necks to see past the crowd huddled around the encased portrait, they, mission accomplished, headed off to buy postcards or find the restroom.

Similarly, most spiritual seekers today are looking for only the most obvious spiritual signs and are missing God's everyday treasures along the way (a lesson best exemplified in the community's partaking of the Lord's Supper). A church ministers to people through its ordinary existence—functioning as a kind of docent for the Holy Spirit, drawing attention to the Spirit for those who are too busy, burdened, or preoccupied to notice. This means that we befriend others on their spiritual journey and offer them biblical wisdom and spiritual insight.

For Paul, there is both an ability and a responsibility for Christians: since (having received the Spirit) we are "spiritual," we are able to discern spiritual things and to interpret them to unbelievers with the wisdom "taught by the Spirit" (1 Cor. 2:12–16). This "public" ministry of discernment is to humbly offer perspective (the docent's job of helping others to "see" something better) to people who are trying to understand what it is they are seeking. As such, it is a witness similar to Paul's speech at Mars Hill, where he reveals to the seeking Athenians the identity of the "unknown God." Using the words of their own culture, Paul affirms that the God they seek is "not far from each one of us" and is indeed calling them to "repent" and trust in the witness of the resurrected Jesus (Acts 17:22–31).[4]

Further, docents of the Spirit help people determine whether it is the Holy Spirit that is present or some other spirit. In this way, it is again a perichoretic activity, asking questions about God's activity in the world within a trinitarian framework: Is this spirit the Spirit of the Father or the Spirit of the Son? Is it the Holy Spirit or some other spirit? Is it merely human enthusiasm or will or, worse yet, a demonic spirit sowing evil (1 Thess. 5:19–22)?

The ministry of being docents of the Spirit is both a type of "worldly" spiritual direction and a witness to the world that the Spirit given to the community (living "within" believers) is also the Spirit at work in the world, drawing people into communion with God. Yet the church plays a crucial role as interpreter of that work, helping unbelievers recognize that their life activity is part of God's activity. This can encourage the unbeliever to continue to recognize God's prompting and respond to it by "seeing" the presence of God not only working with him or her but, in fact, seeking seekers in everyday life (Gen. 3:9; Hosea 3:1–5; Ezek. 34:6, 11–16).[5]

For many Christians who feel obliged by but not comfortable with the concept of "witnessing" or "sharing our faith," the ministry of being a docent of the Spirit means that we see our church community as having a perspective to offer to seekers. We then try to give not so much information as an invitation—to humbly offer our services as a community of people who try to live each day recognizing and responding to God's Spirit at work in the world, thereby encouraging even seekers to see the evidence of God already at work in their lives and thereby calling for a response.

In our church in San Clemente, we intentionally frame most of our "life-stage" classes and seminars to offer a Christian perspective on everything from parenting skills to dealing with depression to the cultural messages given to girls about their body image. We see these classes as not only giving information, but also helping seekers and believers to see the difference between the "spirit of the age" and the Holy Spirit. In a postmodern age in which every experience has a right to be heard, we believe that we can humbly and confidently offer the perspective of what the church has experienced for centuries.

A Host at Every Table

A community that witnesses to the divine communion then bears the love of God to people, points to the work of the Spirit in people's lives, and most important, extends itself in hospitality. All ministry, if it is to be a witness to the divine communion, must have an initiating, welcoming, embracing character reflective of the one who "while we were still sinners, died for us"(Rom. 5:8).[6]

This hospitality must intentionally include others in the community—even before they believe. In his book *The Celtic Way of Evangelism,* George Hunter demonstrates that the effectiveness of St. Patrick's ministry to ancient Ireland was built upon his establishing ministering communities that placed belonging before believing.[7] Seekers were welcomed into the community and were invited to partake of all the ministry therein. The communities believed not only that the act of including the seeker would surround them with love, but that the community's life itself would be the most clear and "vocal" proclamation.

At SCPC, while a person must be a confessing Christian in order to officially join our church (or present children to be baptized), we make clear over and over again that all are welcome and may partake of our ministries and make this their "home" regardless of where they are on the spiritual journey. While many churches would have such an approach, we try to make it a conscious and stated part of our mission. So not only do we offer our church services and programs but, in a world filled with people on spiritual journeys, we aim to offer hospitality that recapitulates God's hospitality—as it is discovered in the Trinity—in the world. As Miroslav Volf writes, "God's reception of hostile humanity into divine communion is a model for how human beings should relate to the other."[8]

While it's not our responsibility to get people to enter into relationship with God, we do have a responsibility to participate in God's activity of inviting and welcoming people into the divine communion. Following the language about families in 1 Corinthians 7:14, Ray Anderson redefines sanctification as consecration, which he defines as "holiness that sanctifies by an act of inclusion rather than by a principle of exclusion." It's "holiness through belonging."[9] Our lives are to be a ministry of consecration, sanctifying people through inclusion, and one way Christians can do this is by incarnating the hospitality of God in all situations.

This concept of being a "host at every table" allows the people of the church to see themselves as placed by God in every situation to reveal the presence of God. Since the communion of the Trinity is not passive, waiting for seekers to "stand at the door and knock," but instead, like Jesus who came to us, extends into the world in redemptive, suffering love,[10] believers follow Christ in extending hospitality to others.

In our San Clemente congregation, we have begun to do this by breaking into neighborhood groupings of fifteen to twenty families that we call neighborhood parishes. The congregation has selected a lay minister to serve each neighborhood. The lay minister's responsibilities are simple and yet profound: start by ensuring that every family in the neighborhood knows every other one and feels comfortable calling on them for support and friendship. Then begin to offer the same care to others in your neighborhood, whether they are church members or not.

Our neighborhood ministries have occasional social gatherings to get to know one another, and the lay ministers know that they are the channel of resources and the connection between the neighborhood and the organized church. If there is a need in the neighborhood, then the lay ministers are trained to encourage neighbors to provide meals, offer support, pray, and call upon the pastors, if necessary. We tell the lay ministers, "Your job is not just to care for all the Presbyterians, but to get the Presbyterians caring for all their neighbors." Whether a person ever comes on our campus or not, we want that person to experience the love of God coming to him or her. In loving each other and then others in the neighborhood, the church offers hospitality to everyone, committing to follow our Lord in extending that fellowship to even the most unlikely, trusting that transformations will take place because we did.

Whether it is risking asking to dinner a Zacchaeus or a stranger we met on the road, we trust that Christ will reveal himself in the breaking of bread (Luke 24) in whatever conversation, business transaction, leisurely gathering, reunion of friends, or reconciliation of differences. Whether it be a kitchen table where a friend shares a burden over coffee, a boardroom table where a company's strategic plans are confirmed, or a courtroom table where justice is sought, to the Christian these tables can become "communion tables" where Jesus' own inclusive love is offered. Our responsibility is to have the mindset of a servant, representing Christ, who is always, though often unacknowledged, the host of the gathering and the one inviting every person into the life-transforming communion.

The Witness That Transforms

As bearers of divine love, docents of the Spirit, and hosts at every table, we participate in the glorifying of God together in a way that also changes us. As we live out the transforming witness through prayer, discernment, and ministry, we not only find that we are faithful witnesses to God, but we begin to take on the "exceptional life" that is the most effective response to seekers. In this perichoretic activity of God, we both pray and are changed by praying, discern and are changed by discerning, glorify God and are changed into people of glory by ministering. As the increasingly exceptional quality of our lives is revealed, God also is increasingly revealed.

As we allow our eyes to turn from the divine figures in Rublev's icon to the ministry cup in the center, what we have learned is that while each of us is called to share the fellowship and fate of Jesus, for the world to see that exceptional life that is a witness to a seeking world, all of us as a community of believers must share the cup indeed. As we seek to reveal a perfect Triune God, we too learn the lesson that Billy Chapel learned in love and baseball—no one is perfect alone.

Conclusion

People of the Table

A Spirituality of Fellowship and Following

A few years ago, a young couple came to my office to have their son baptized. My predecessor had baptized their daughter some years earlier. They had attended church for a while and even considered joining it formally but grew disillusioned during a time of congregational turmoil. Now, meeting with me and answering the baptismal questions, it became apparent that while the mother could affirm an undeveloped but sincere Christian faith, the father really could not. When I gently probed further, I found that the father was really quite skeptical of any organized religion. He told me that he had "found peace in family and the ocean." But he also wanted his children to have a "traditional base" from which to operate. Without directly saying so, he wanted his son baptized because he believed that we should start in a tradition and then grow into individual experiences of God and self that we find on our own. Why isn't that kind of self-made spirituality enough? he wondered. Why do I need to confess allegiance to Christ and be part of the church?

Hopefully, by now you have an answer for this earnest seeker. Why do we need to be part of the community? Because the community is a reflection of the image of God, and only within the community can we become what we were made for. True spiritual life is found only in the People of the Table.

A Return to the Table in the Coffee Shop

As noted at the outset, I've imagined this book as a conversation with different "representatives" sitting around a table at a coffee shop. John Calvin and theologians of past and present have had ample time to push the conversation in a historically and theologically rooted direction. The spiritual writers of today and the church strategists have been affirmed and appreciated for contributing vibrant spiritual formation practices and sociologically perceptive evangelism techniques, but they have also been challenged to ground both spiritual disciplines and ministry systems in a far more communal and intentionally *churchly* framework. If nothing else, they will need to reconsider the place of the one clear activity given to us by our Lord for both edifying our faith community and demonstrating the gospel: the community of God.

My intention has been to correct an oversight in vibrant evangelical theology: *a weak ecclesiology*. Through the conversation we have tried to recover a central truth that is necessary for being the kind of community that can form exceptional people: *As God is, so the church should be. As God does, the church should do.* With the result being that *the more the church is like God, the more individual souls will become like Christ*.

But what about the "seekers"? Do *the people of the Table* truly have anything to offer those who are already so disillusioned by Christians and the church? If Acts 2 has any power today, then we have to say yes. For a return to the community life of the earliest Christians—a life devoted to the Word, prayers and meals together, a life of praising God, and much time together led then—and I believe now—to the church "having the goodwill of all the people" and more and more "added to their number those who were being saved."

But we can't minimize the challenge that seekers pose. Maybe the most telling commentary about the current interest in spirituality is found in the lead-in to Kenneth Woodward's *Newsweek* article: "Americans love the search so much that the idea of a destination is lost."[1] It's this struggle between unfocused spiritual pursuit and spiritual pursuit with a clear destination that separates the current "trend" from the centuries-old spiritual hunger of believers everywhere.

For this reason, Robert Wuthnow cautions us against trying to reestablish spirituality as necessarily connected to any physical or geographic structure (what he calls a "dwelling-oriented spirituality").[2] For him, that spirituality of two generations ago and before has gone. Societal changes have disconnected us from dwelling spaces, farms, family, homes, and, yes, churches. We may not be happy about it, but we are now a culture of seekers, many even taking pride in being spiritually homeless. Tying spirituality exclusively to any sense of space, structure, or tradition is irrelevant to those who are looking for God. They will no more show up at a church to find out "what Presbyterians believe" than they will take a trip to check out the latest findings of the Phrenology Fellowship. And while many in our culture long and even work for creating a new sense of "community," trying to anchor that community in any space is increasingly difficult amid the pervasive feelings of rootlessness that grip our culture.[3]

But Wuthnow also warns us not to throw in the towel and make Christian faith just another highly personalized self-constructed spirituality so common today (what he calls "seeker-oriented spirituality").[4] Instead, he suggests that a spirituality grounded in a people who share the same values and disciplines has a chance to offer a clear choice (what he calls "practice-oriented spirituality") based on their commitments.

If the seekers of our era are genuinely less interested in sacred places than were women and men of centuries past, then it could be argued that *the most impressive cathedrals of the future will be not mere buildings, but rather vibrant communities of God's redeemed people.* While churches in our culture will always need sanctuaries and facilities (and indeed, our church in San Clemente is in the midst of what will be a decade-long, massive building campaign), we now see the necessity for investing even more in the church as a *community.* If the church is going to produce the kinds of exceptional people who provide a satisfying and attractive example to a watching world, then our Christian faith must be more deliberately, intentionally, and inextricably *communal*.

For those of us who lead churches, there is both a clear call and an opportunity here. While there may no longer be a strong sense of sacred *space*, community calls us to see our mission as focused first and foremost on a people in a particular *place*. To that end, let me suggest that the old monastic vow of *stability* needs to be reconsidered in some form. Pastors who are busy climbing ecclesial ladders should well reconsider the value of long (maybe even lifelong or career-long) tenures in one church. Denominations who move pastors from one parish to another should reflect upon whether organizational instability is holding back the opportunity for some local congregations to thrive over a long period of time. Seminaries need to equip pastors for the spiritual and psychological requirements of a long, healthy pastorate. How can pastors build a truly life-transforming community if they are changing jobs every three to five years?

Second, as church leaders—both clergy and laity—see their call as "community-builders" who are helping to shape holy and healthy churches as the life-transforming center of exceptional living, they necessarily face the challenge of living out the vision of a God who is Communion. From that vision comes the responsibility of ensuring that all the central activities of the church reinforce and "enculturate" members as a community of people who embody God's own character in the world.

Last, if the community is the witness to the world, then the stale debate about "ministry vs. mission" or "what we spend on *us* vs. what we give to mission" is over. Yes, there will always be need and demand for churches to eagerly and generously join together in furthering the work of the mission of God in the world. Yes, there will always be a necessity to *send out* missionaries and to send resources to areas where the resources are limited. But if the community of God's people is in fact the witness of God, the mission of God, to a particular location, then the people of God are *the sent ones* as a community, the mission of God is right before us, and our post-Christian, postmodern, seeking world is our mission field, wherever we are.[5]

That sense of mission to the seekers of the world gives our communities an even more urgent reason for being. We must—*by the way we live together*—affirm the reality of who God is as Divine Communion, and model our lives on God's life. That "witness by living together" calls forth a spirituality to be lived out in our larger communities. We are not only messengers of the gospel; we are, by our lives together, the very mission of God who is at work in the world.

As Christians, our life is founded on the Divine Communion of God gathered around the eternal table brought into the world. That life is celebrated and enriched through the most ordinary of rituals ever given to humanity: eating bread and drinking wine. And finally, that life is extended into the world so that the most ordinary events of life, events expressed metaphorically at every table in every home, every office, and every school or public gathering place, are opportunities to encounter the God who is love who has come into the world. We must be from first to last, *the people of the Table* expressing and living out a truly life-transforming spirituality of *fellowship and following*.

Fellowship and Following

A spirituality of *fellowship and following* is firmly oriented within the biblical vision of a *people of God* who are on a journey *with* God, expressing the reign of God, following God in trust and obedience and being transformed into the likeness of the Triune God in process. Further it is *an obedient response* to the invitation into communion with God that the Bible refers to as "following," and is expressed in a specific fellowship of followers. We find this theme—being called by God into fellowship and then following God in obedience—grounded biblically in God's call to Abram (Gen. 12), Israel's journey from Egypt to the promised land (Exodus), the instructions to "follow God" and be his own people (Deut. 5:1–6:25; Lev. 26:3, 12–13), and especially in Jesus' call to his disciple (Matt. 4 and parallels) and assurance that those who follow him will be with him (John 10, 14–17, see also Matt. 8:2; Mark 1:17; John 13:36). These texts remind us that the destination of the spiritual pursuit is not ultimately a sacred place but a Person, not a "where" but a "Who."

As Augustine reminds us in his famous prayer from his *Confessions*, "O God, Thou hast made us for Thyself, and our hearts are restless until they rest in Thee." The source of soul's rest is not what we can earn or buy or achieve, but the union of the believer with Christ.[6] The "destination" of the spiritual quest is the conformity of that believer into the likeness of Christ, through that union.[7] Fellowship with a communal God is expressed by following God. Such a spirituality of fellowship and following offers both the spiritually homeless a home (albeit with a "nomadic" spiritual people) and the spiritually seeking a path of discipline, guidance, and connection to something outside oneself. Ultimately, it offers the fulfillment of God's intention in creating human beings, that we all would be transformed into the divine image.

The Hunger to Be Changed

This trinitarian spirituality of fellowship and following both *connects to and challenges* the cultural and theological situation we face today. It connects to the challenge of the seeker: first, by acknowledging the hunger to *become* something different. It speaks to the one who is searching by offering a language of transformation through "nurture"[8]—in a way that addresses the human need to develop through relationship and love. Further, *fellowship and following* engages the rootlessness of society by offering a spirituality of *belonging*. It is an expression of the Trinity that is an open communion reaching out to the world in the embrace of divine love. Transformation through relationship with God and other followers of Jesus Christ is at the heart of this.

We find in it an echo of Calvin's famous definition of "true and sound wisdom" as the knowledge of self and God, understood not as "knowledge about" but knowledge through relationship[9] bringing together the personal and the communal experience. In this way, it is grounded in the Hebrew Scripture's view of discipleship. According to Rabbi Michael Goldberg, discipleship is an intentionally personal activity of one person who is in relationship to a teacher. In direct contrast to the modern, detached, rationalistic academic approach, "arriving at the truth as traditionally understood by Jews and Christians, has hinged not so much on following a method but following the lives of other human beings."[10]

With its focus on becoming and belonging, this spirituality also offers the seeker a sense of *purpose and a wisdom for living purposefully.* As one embraced in transforming communion, a person engaged in *fellowship and following* necessarily engages the world and responds to its needs and cries with the example and power of Jesus the Communion incarnate. But, as a result of the further incarnation of the Holy Spirit as the body of Christ, it is not simply a set of beliefs, but a *habitus*, a wisdom for sacramentally living in the world. The outcome is people who bear divine love, offer hospitality, and build community, who serve as docents of the Holy Spirit, who discern, witness to, and reveal in the ordinary circumstances of life the very presence of the Triune God "'in [whom] we live and move and have our being'" (Acts 17:28). It understands that the gift of the Spirit to the church is the true *mysterium* or sacrament,[11] and that the purpose of the people of God is quintessentially revealed in the simple activity of eating bread and drinking wine as they "proclaim the Lord's death" (1 Cor. 11:26). This everyday communal action is a model of how all of our everyday experiences are to be a proclamation of God's presence and call.

However, this trinitarian spirituality of fellowship and following responds to the challenge of the seeker by also *offering a counterchallenge*. Like the God who questions the questioner (Job 28:3; Luke 20:3), the Triune God challenges the seeker to find full humanity through *repentance, not fulfillment*. The seeker is challenged to accept that *true becoming begins with baptism* in the name of the Father, Son, and Holy Spirit and being joined into the life of the Triune God. Baptism expresses both God's embrace and our submission. As God's activity, it is the loving welcome into the covenant; as something we *undergo,* it demands humility that calls us beyond spiritual self-expression. As Ellen Charry has written, "Christian identity is neither self-made nor constructed from the narrative of one's personal history or biology."[12] This is a cause for celebration, she notes. "It means that one is never alone but always accompanied by the Holy Spirit and the fullness of the Trinity itself."[13] But it is also a confrontation, calling the seeker to ground his or her search in a relationship and a tradition, both requiring commitment.[14]

From this we see that such a spirituality is also a challenge to a world where the "formation of the self has been overshadowed by the emancipation of the self."[15] Seekers are confronted with a spirituality that is both gift and demand. The Triune God offers fellowship to all who would accept it freely, but the cost of following is a life of repentance. The gift of fellowship is given to empower the following; the promised presence of God makes certain the fulfilling of God's purposes (Phil. 1:6), but instead of self-satisfaction, self-actualization, or self-realization, this involves the utter transformation of one's whole self so as to become like God (Rom. 8:29).

Miroslav Volf describes this as changing self-centered people into "de-centered centers," those who have been embraced by God in the fellowship of the Trinity and have had their old self-centered nature "crucified with Christ" (Gal. 2:19–20) and are now able to demonstrate through their lives the presence of the God whose *essence* is "perichoresis of their love" (1 John 3:16, 4:7–12).[16] Seekers must seek in order to become; to become we must change, and to change we must die to our old selves and find our new life in the transforming communion of God.

This spirituality not only connects to the seeker by offering belonging, but also challenges the seeker by *demanding fellowship*. Spirituality is not about making a solo ascent but about becoming part of a community modeled on God-Who-Is-Communion, that is constituted by the Word as Scripture and sacrament. This spirituality challenges the individualism that is so rooted in both the culture and the church,[17] as well as seekers' and believers' tendency to create fellowship according to their own image.

Return for a minute to the story of the young unbelieving dad who brought his son to be baptized. While he wanted a church to simply codify his own privatized spiritual journey, a spirituality of *fellowship and following* both affirms his yearnings and challenges him to find true fulfillment beyond himself. It acknowledges the reality of God present in creation and in family. It empathizes with the restlessness of the soul yearning for "peace," and it criticizes institutional forms of faith that are devoid of the spirit of community and the wonder of creation.

Yet it also challenges the common temptation to limit spirituality to "inspiration," to believe that the end is only a personal, even private, experience. Instead, *fellowship and following* affirms inspiration as God's address and then tutors the inspired response. It recognizes creation and family (and many other things) as common grace or points of contact that are not the end but the means to a life of trust and following God. Finding ourselves affirmed and approached by God, we are inspired to leave self-centeredness behind and enter the fellowship constituted by the Triune God, expressing our spirituality in sacrificial, self-giving love.

When that father asked me why he needed to be in church to worship, my response was that he had confused inspiration with worship. We are inspired by ocean waves and a child's gaze, but we respond to that inspiration by following God and worshiping him as he has told us to: as part of the community of his people.

Finally, this spirituality connects to the seeker by being a spirituality of everyday life but also challenges such a person to view it as involving Christ as Lord of all life, including his or her own. There is no arena where Christ is not Lord, no place where the love and truth of the Triune God does not extend, no part of life hidden from God. It not only invites us to participate in the world, but also demands that we do so as part of our spirituality.

Picking Up the Gauntlet

From the outset, I've reflected on Martyn Lloyd-Jones's assertion a generation ago that the way to meet the challenge of spiritual seekers today is through our exceptional living. I contend that we pick up the gauntlet, not by seeking to accommodate self-centered spiritual seekers, but to connect to and challenge them with lives that embody the transforming communion of God. To that end, this book has been a spiritual theology *for Christian communities* who want to develop people whose lives reflect God and answer the challenge of the world. Because of this, the central "disciplines" of this spirituality are communal: worship, Word, and witness. And our spirituality is for the twofold purpose of our own transformation and revealing God's glory to others. We must hold before us the vision of Zechariah, where God's presence is so evident amid the people that spiritual seekers from every background and nationality will take hold of the garments of one believer who is simply gathering

with God's people in worship and declare, "Let us go with you, for we have heard that God is with you" (Zech. 8:23).

With this before us, it is imperative to recognize that while a spirituality of fellowship and following is a point of engagement with seekers, we do *not* offer a "spirituality of fellowship and following" to the world directly. We offer God. We proclaim and demonstrate the good news of God's present availability and reign in Jesus Christ through the Holy Spirit. We do not offer spiritual seekers a different spirituality; we offer them the very presence of God that has embraced us in the transforming communion of the Trinity, calls us to live in the transforming communion of the church and sends us into the world as the extension of God's transforming communion. In this way, the Christian church is obedient to the Father, Son, and Holy Spirit who are revealed in the Scriptures and in our own lives. We do this to the end that the follower of Christ becomes like Christ, who himself was the image of the Triune God. In this way, Christians enjoy and display together an "exceptional life"—one that changes them and their loved ones, one that commends itself to millions of seekers longing to find their places at the table of the family of God. That, I believe, is both something quite exceptional and something exceptional to offer a seeking world.

Notes

Introduction

1. David K. Winecoff, "Calvin's Doctrine of Mortification," *Presbyterion: Covenant Seminary Review* 13:2 (fall 1987), 85.

2. See Dallas Willard, *The Spirit of the Disciplines: Understanding How God Changes Lives* (San Francisco: HarperSanFrancisco, 1999); Willard, *The Divine Conspiracy* (San Francisco: HarperSanFrancisco, 1998); and Simon Chan, *Spiritual Theology: A Systematic Study of the Christian Life* (Downers Grove, Ill.: InterVarsity Press, 1998).

3. See Rick Warren, *The Purpose Driven Church* (Grand Rapids: Zondervan, 1995); Robert Lewis, *The Church of Irresistible Influence* (Grand Rapids: Zondervan, 2001); Randy Frazee, *The Connecting Church* (Grand Rapids: Zondervan, 2001).

4. Emil Brunner, *The Misunderstanding of the Church* (Philadelphia: Westminster, 1953), 12.

5. See Robert Wuthnow (ed.), *I Come Away Stronger: How Small Groups are Shaping American Religion* (Grand Rapids: Eerdmans, 1994); Wuthnow, *After Heaven: Spirituality in America since the 1950s* (Berkeley and Los Angeles: University of California Press, 1998); and Frazee, *The Connecting Church*.

6. Robert Wuthnow, *Sharing the Journey: Support Groups and America's New Quest for Community* (New York: Free Press, 1994), 358. Wuthnow described the ethos of the small group as a collection of individuals committed to the group because each of them would say, "I come away stronger."

7. Dietrich Bonhoeffer, *Christ the Center* (New York: Harper and Row, 1960), 60. "The community is therefore, not only the receiver of the Word of revelation; it is itself revelation. . . . The community is the body of Christ. Body here is not just a metaphor. The community *is* the body of Christ; it does not *represent* the Body of Christ."

8. G. C. Berkouwer, *Faith and Sanctification*, trans. John Vriend (Grand Rapids: Eerdmans, 1952), 10–11.

9. A picture of Rublev's icon can be found at www.auburn.edu/academic/liberal_arts/foreign/russian/icons/trinity-rublev.html.

Chapter 1

1. Peter F. Drucker, *Managing Non-Profit Organizations* (San Francisco: Harper Business, 1990).

2. *The Book of Order of the Presbyterian Church (USA)* (Louisville: Geneva Press, 1997) G-3.0200.

Chapter 2

1. D. Martyn Lloyd-Jones, "Review of G. C. Berkouwer's *Faith and Sanctification*," *Evangelical Quarterly* 25 (April 1953), 107.

2. Dietrich Bonhoeffer, *Sanctorum Communio* (London: Collins, 1957), 160: "The church is 'Christ existing as community.'"

3. See Leonard Sweet, *SoulTsunami* (Grand Rapids: Zondervan, 1999), 408–19. Sweet offers another recap of the pervasive and growing interest in spirituality in Western culture.

4. Kenneth L. Woodward, "On the Road Again," *Newsweek*, November 28, 1994, 61. *Newsweek* chronicled a pervasive interest in spirituality within American popular culture. And the trend only increased throughout the decade.

5. Woodward, "On the Road Again," 61. This renewed attention to spirituality is not limited to popular culture, being increasingly evident among academics also. For a lengthy and multifaceted discussion of spirituality as an academic discipline and churchly discussion, see Bradley C. Hanson, ed., *Modern Christian Spirituality: Methodological and Historical Essay* (Atlanta: Scholars Press of the American Academy of Religion, 1990).

6. Robert Wuthnow, *After Heaven: Spirituality in America since the 1950s* (Berkeley and Los Angeles: University of California Press, 1998),12. Cf. Elizabeth Lesser, *The New American Spirituality: A Seeker's Guide* (New York: Random House, 1999), xvii. Lesser develops her guide to spirituality from the concept that democracy has freed spiritual seekers to define spirituality any way they choose: "America is just the place for spiritual seekers to be lamps unto themselves."

7. Sweet, *SoulTsunami*, 409. See also Tom Beaudoin, *Virtual Faith: The Irreverent Spiritual Quest of Generation X* (San Francisco: Jossey-Bass, 1998).

8. *Barna Report*, March 8, 1999, from website www.barna.org.

9. See George Gallup Jr., *Religion in America 1992–93* (Princeton: Princeton Research Center, 1993), 21. According to Gallup, only 4 percent of the "unchurched" skip church because they don't believe in God. See also William Hendricks, *Exit Interviews* (Chicago: Moody, 1993), 250; Wade Clark Roof, *A Generation of Seekers: The Spiritual Journeys of the Baby Boom Generation* (San Francisco: HarperSanFrancisco, 1993), 76–77. See especially, George Barna, *Understanding Ministry in a Changing Culture* (Glendale, Calif.: Barna Research Group, 1993), 90: "49 percent of the unchurched say that having a close relationship with God is very desirable, [but] only 13 percent say that being part of a local church is very desirable." *The Barna Report,* February 25, 1999, "One Out of Three Adults Is Now Unchurched" (from website, www.barna.org), confirms that this is the continuation of a pattern that first emerged more than a decade ago." See also George Gallup Jr. and Jim Castelli, *The People's Religion: American Faith in the '90s* (New York: Macmillan, 1989), 44, 90: "[There is] a clear increase in the level of interest in religion despite the increase in unchurched Americans and those professing no religious affiliation. . . . Americans are increasingly divorcing their personal religious behavior from their attitudes toward organized religion." Americans "tend to view their churches less as sources of faith than as resources for their personal and family religious and spiritual needs."

10. In his seminar address, "Spiritual Formation in Christ: A Perspective on What It Is and How It Might Be Done," given at Fuller Theological Seminary, October 22, 1993, on the occasion of the inauguration of Richard J. Mouw as president, Dallas Willard said, "I believe that 'spirituality' is the arena in which evangelical faith and practice will have to struggle desperately, in the coming years to retain its integrity, as all 'spiritualities' present themselves as equal—under slogans such as 'interfaith' and 'ecumenism,' which increasingly apply to all religious cultures and not just to the branches of Christianity." A similar description is offered and conclusion drawn by Wuthnow, *After Heaven,* 13.

11. George Gallup Jr. and Jim Castelli, *The People's Religion: American Faith in the 90's* (New York: MacMillan, 1989), 252. In answering a question about what the church could do to build greater interest in religion in the coming years, the second highest response (behind only "better communication" between laity and institutions and among individuals) was "concentrate more on religion," a call, according to the authors for greater emphasis on spirituality. See also *George Barna Reports,* March 8, 1999, "Annual Survey of America's Faith Shows No Significant Changes in Past Year," and February 25, 1999, "One Out of Three Adults Is Now Unchurched."

12. This widely acknowledged decline has been charted by many demographers. See Gallup and Castelli, *People's Religion,* 265. Cf. "Annual Survey of America's Faith."

13. Gallup and Castelli, *People's Religion,* 21. The authors have identified three "gaps" in American Christianity: (1) *the knowledge gap*: the gap between a person's stated belief and his or her knowledge of those beliefs, (2) *the ethics gap*: the gap between the degree of stated convictions and their consistency in living them out, and (3) *the Believers vs. Belongers gap*: the gap between the rise in spiritual interest and the decrease in involvement with organized religion. See also Robert Wuthnow, *God and Mammon in America* (New York: Free Press, 1994). Wuthnow charts the fact that there is little difference in churched and unchurched attitudes and decisions about money, work, and materialism, as well as levels of anxiety about financial concerns.

14. Willard, "Spiritual Formation in Christ."

15. Richard Lovelace, "The Sanctification Gap," *Theology Today* 29 (1973), 365–66. See also Ellen Charry, *By the Renewing of Your Minds: The Pastoral Function of Christian Doctrine* (New York: Oxford University Press, 1997), vii.

16. See Edward Farley, *Theologia: The Fragmentation and Unity of Theological Education* (Philadelphia: Fortress, 1983).

17. Richard B. Hays, *The Moral Vision of the New Testament: Community, Cross, New Creation* (San Francisco: HarperCollins, 1996), 196.

18. Rodney Clapp, "On the Making of Kings and Christians: Worship and Christian Formation," in Todd E. Johnson, ed., *The Conviction of Things Not Seen: Worship and Ministry in the 21st Century* (Grand Rapids: Brazos, 2002), 113–14.

19. Lovelace, "The Sanctification Gap," 365. Lovelace attributes some of the "gap" to the fact that the "historical development of Protestant evangelicalism has predisposed it to lose sight of the central importance of sanctification." He also asserts that the tendency of the hyper-Calvinism of the post-Puritans was to overload the content of justification. This, then, led to a reaction in the revival theology of Charles Finney and his contemporaries. This, in turn, led "conservatives" (as opposed to late nineteenth-century and early twentieth-century "liberal" theologians, who were more engaged in making the Christian message palatable to modern tastes) to engage in a lengthy preoccupation with the doctrine of justification. The result was a neglect of the doctrine of sanctification in both "liberal" and "conservative" circles. As I will demonstrate in a later chapter, sanctification through the church was at the center of Calvin's theology.

20. According to Edward Farley, the training of pastors was historically about training seminarians in the wisdom to apply spiritual insights to everyday life. But over time, theological education changed. What was once about forming pastors to form Christian communities to form Christian souls, eventually became "sociological professionalism" of highly technical ministry activities. The result is that while ministers may be more professionally competent as counselors, educators, and administrators, they are less equipped to preach, teach, form, and lead communities that form exceptional people.

21. James M. Houston, "Spirituality," *Evangelical Dictionary of Theology,* ed. Walter Elwell (Grand Rapids: Baker, 1984), 1050.

22. For a thorough study of the pervasive causes and effects of nominal Christianity, see Eddie Gibbs, *In Name Only: Tackling the Problem of Nominal Christianity* (Wheaton, Ill.: Victor Books, 1994).

23. Alister McGrath, *Evangelicalism and the Future of Christianity* (Downers Grove, Ill.: InterVarsity Press, 1995), 124. Cf. Stanley J. Grenz, *Revisioning Evangelical Theology: A Fresh Agenda for the 21st Century* (Downers Grove, Ill.: InterVarsity Press, 1993), 37–60.

24. Indeed, George Barna notes that while the interest in spirituality is on the rise, Christianity has shown no demonstrable growth in numbers or influence within the culture (*Barna Report*, March 8, 1999, from website www.barna.org).

25. Hendricks, *Exit Interviews,* 250: "Well, if the unchurched may be far more 'spiritual' than they are usually given credit for, could the reverse also be true—that the 'churched' are actually less 'spiritual' than they are also often assumed to be? Gallup suggests precisely that." Cf. 261.

26. Hendricks, *Exit Interviews,* 261.

27. See Robert J. Banks, *Going to Church in the First Century* (Beaumont: Christian Books, 1992), for a description of an early church gathering and celebration of the Lord's Supper.

28. See comment on 2 Cor 3:18 in John Calvin, *Commentaries of John Calvin,* (Grand Rapids: Calvin Translation Society, 47 volumes, 1948–1981).

Chapter 3

1. Robert Bellah et al. *Habits of the Heart: Individualism and Commitment in American Life,* updated ed. (Berkeley and Los Angeles: University of California Press, 1996).

2. Barry Shain, *The Myth of American Individualism* (Princeton: Princeton University Press, 1994).

3. Robert D. Putnam, *Bowling Alone: The Collapse and Revival of American Community* (Touchstone: New York, 2000).

4. For a provocative study about this and other themes in this book, see William Dyrness, *How America Hears the Gospel* (Grand Rapids: Eerdmans, 1989). In chapter 4, "Virgin Land," Dyrness describes how the "frontier mentality" of early Americans has contributed to a pervasive "pilgrim" motif, as well as to a value for the solitary "traveler."

5. See Ellen Charry, *By the Renewing of Your Minds: The Pastoral Function of Christian Doctrine* (New York: Oxford University Press, 1997), 199: "If we take doctrine and piety as two separate fields, one academic and the other pastoral, we will never understand Calvin." Charry describes Calvin, in her term, as an "aretegenically oriented teacher of the church who understands the implication of theology for public life." That is, that Calvin's teaching was not simply to assert Christian truth, but also to form virtuous lives.

6. John Calvin, *Institutes of the Christian Religion,* 2 vols., ed. J. T. McNeil and trans. F. L. Battles, Library of Christian Classics 20–21 (Philadelphia: Westminster, 1960),1.15.6.

Cf. *Inst.* 1.15.7 where Calvin argues that "suitable for our present purposes" (i.e., "the upbuilding of godliness") there is not needed further discussion of the "minutiae of Aristotle," which "entangle ourselves in useless questions." Instead he gives a simple definition of the faculties of the soul. Cf. Langdon Gilkey, *Reaping the Whirlwind: A Christian Interpretation of History* (New York: Seabury, 1976), 177: "Calvin is, therefore, interested in doctrines solely insofar as they provide the grounds for piety, a symbolic framework for faithful obedience."

7. John Calvin, *Institutes.* See Calvin's prefatory address to King Francis I in the 1536 edition, reiterated in the 1559 edition with similar language.

8. The entire paradigm of sanctification is based around Matthew 16:24 and parallels in Calvin, *Commentary.*

9. See Calvin's *Commentary* on John 13:15. See also *Comm.* 1 John 2:6: "Yet he does not simply exhort us to imitate Christ; but from the union we have with him, he proves that we ought to be like him." See also *Comm.* 1 Pe. 2:21, 1 Pe. 4:1.

10. In note 35 in *Inst.* 2.2.6 the sophists are identified as "Ockham and his later interpreters such as Gabriel Biel and the Sorbonne theologians of his own day."

11. Commenting on "renewing of one's mind" in Romans 12:1–2, Calvin says, "[The moral philosophers] set up reason alone as the ruling principle in man and they think that it alone should be listened to; to it alone, in short, they entrust the conduct of life. But the Christian philosophy bids reason give way to, submit and subject itself to, the Holy Spirit so that the man himself no longer lives but hears Christ reigning and living within him" (*Inst.* 3.7.1).

12. *Inst.* 3.7.1. In a note on the preface for the 1560 edition, the editor writes: "Calvin in 3.7.1 sharply distinguishes the 'Christian philosophy' from that of the 'philosophers' as a life not ordered according to reason alone but renewed in Christ and directed by the Holy Spirit."

13. *Inst.* 1.5.9: "According to Calvin, real knowledge of God is "not that knowledge which, content with empty speculation, merely flits in the brain, but that which will be sound and fruitful if we duly perceive it and if it takes root in the heart."

14. *Inst.* 3.6.4. Cf. William J. Bouwsma, "The Spirituality of John Calvin" in Jill Raitt, ed. *Christian Spirituality II: High Middle Ages and Reformation,* vol.17 of *World Spirituality: An Encyclopedic History of the Religious Quest* (New York: Crossroad, 1987), 327.

15. Which Calvin says that God gives to them as a "slight taste of divinity that they might not hide their impiety under a cloak of ignorance" (*Inst.* 2.2.18).

16. *Inst.* 2.2.18.

17. *Inst.* 3.6.3.

18. *Inst.* 3.3.3.

19. *Inst.* 3.2.24. Cf. *Comm.* 2 Cor. 3:18: "God makes his glory shine forth in us little by little."

20. Calvin, *Inst.*, 3.1.1; cf. 2.16.19; 3.24.5. Cf. *Comm.* Rom. 8:13. L. Berkhof, *Systematic Theology,* 447; Sinclair Ferguson, "Reformed Spirituality" in Donald L. Alexander, *Christian Spirituality: Five Views of Sanctification* (Downers Grove, Ill.: InterVarsity Press, 1988), 34. Ferguson sees union with Christ as at the center of both justification and sanctification in Calvin (citing *Inst.* 2.16.9). He also refers to B. B. Warfield: "It is not faith that saves, but Christ who saves through faith."

21. Calvin, *Comm.*, Gala. 3:27. Commenting on "As many of you as have been baptized into Christ have put on Christ," Calvin writes: "[Paul], therefore, explains, in a few words, what is implied in our being united, or rather, made one with the Son of God. . . . He means that they are so closely united to him that in the presence of God, they bear

the name and character of Christ, and are viewed in him rather than in themselves." L. Berkhof (*Systematic Theology*, 452) misses this point when he separates "mystical union" from justification (see below).

22. Ronald S. Wallace, *Calvin, Geneva, and the Reformation* (Grand Rapids: Baker, 1988), 67: "Our conformity with Christ depends on union rather than on imitation."

23. For Protestant thinkers, the concept of mystical union came under suspicion because of its Catholic associations, where grace is an infusion of a substance into the nature of the believer. Furthermore, within Catholic theology, mystical union has a hierarchical aspect: it speaks of a "relationship between a person and God in the *highest degrees* of mystical life (Cf. *New Catholic Encyclopedia* [Washington, D.C.: Catholic University of America, 1967], vol.10, 174.). It is at these two crucial points, the nature of the union and the idea of hierarchy, where Calvin's view of mystical union differs greatly from the commonly accepted Catholic view. While Catholic theology posits a transmission of properties between God and us, for Calvin there exists no diminishment of individuality, no commingling of divine and human properties, no absorption of the human into Christ, but "the relationship with Christ is none the less of the closest, while allowing of the integral subsistence of the properties of man and those of Christ" (*Inst.* 3.1.1). "We must understand that as long as Christ remains outside of us, and we are separated from him, and all that he has suffered and done for the salvation of the human race remains useless and of no value to us." Cf. François Wendel, *Calvin: Origins and Development of His Religious Thought* (1950, repr., trans. Philip Mairet [Durham: Labyrinth Press, 1987], 235).

24. C. Partee, "Calvin's Central Dogma Again," *Sixteenth Century Journal* 18:2 (summer 1987), 194. Cf. David K. Winecoff, "Calvin's Doctrine of Mortification," *Presbyterion: Covenant Seminary Review* 13:2 (fall 1987), 86.

25. Partee, "Central Dogma," 194; the focus of the *Institutes* "is not on entirely separate entities but on relationships." Cf. Gilkey, *Reaping*, 176.

26. From Calvin's "Ninth Sermon on the Passion," in *Opera Omni Quae Supersunt* 46, 953, cited in Wendel, *Calvin: Origins*, 237.

27. Cf. *Inst.* 3.24.5 where election is understood as "sure communion" given to us by Christ himself. Election is seen in this passage in relational language, i.e., Christ has chosen us to be in communion with him as his body. Our certainty of our sustaining election is our communion with Christ as part of his body, and not anything of ourselves.

28. *Inst.* 4.17.1 Again, the distinction of "one flesh" is a delicate one that needs to be fully understood. Commenting on Ephesians 5:31, "and they two shall be one flesh," which Calvin declares as an "exact quotation of the writings of Moses," he writes, "They shall constitute one person . . . all depends on this, that the wife was formed of the flesh and bones of her husband. Such is the union between us and Christ, who in some sort makes us partakers of his substance. 'We are bone of his bone and flesh of his flesh,' not because like ourselves, he has a human nature, but because by the power of his Holy Spirit, he makes us a part of his body, so that from him we derive our life" (*Comm.* on Eph. 5:31).

29. *Comm.* Eph. 5:32.

30. Cf. *Inst.* 3.1.1: "The Holy Spirit is the bond by which Christ effectively unites us to himself." Cf. *Comm.* John 17:21.

31. *Inst.* 3.11.10.

32. Winecoff, "Calvin's Doctrine of Mortification," 87. Cf. *Comm.* Gal. 2:20; *Comm.* John 13:8; *Comm.* John 17:17. See also *Comm.* Rom. 8:13: "Let then the faithful learn to embrace him, not only for justification, but also for sanctification, as he has been given to us for both of these purposes."

33. Ronald S. Wallace, *Calvin's Doctrine of the Christian Life*, (Grand Rapids: Eerdmans, 1959), 331: "With the increase of faith and the participation of the ordinances of Christ, this union is increased more and more."

34. In a letter to a church in Paris, dated January 28, 1555, Calvin equated the "heavenly life" with the mystical union of believers and the ascended Christ. This "heavenly life" was not a spatial affair, but involved a change in relationships, motivations, loyalties, and goals. Cf. *Comm* Ps. 30:4. See Wallace, *Calvin, Geneva, and the Reformation*, 198: "When we have such communion with (Christ) by the Holy Spirit, Calvin explained, he is not only brought down to us on this Earth, but our souls are also raised up to him so that we can participate here and now in the glory in his ascended life and glory."

35. See *Comm.* 1 Pe. 1:15–16, where Calvin, in teaching about the command to be "holy as God is holy," exhorts the believer to progress in holiness. Calvin's emphasis, however, is clearly seen in the fact that he adds a phrase that is not in the biblical text when he writes: "And we ought to remember that we are not only told what our duty is, but that God also adds, 'I am He who sanctifies you.'" Cf. Wallace *Calvin, Geneva, and the Reformation*, 188: "Through what Calvin calls a 'mystical union' with the exalted Lord who is calling him, [the believer] is *empowered* to offer his life for such self-denial and cross-bearing" (emphasis mine).

36. Stanley Hauerwas, *Character and the Christian Life* (San Antonio: Trinity University Press, 1975), 193.

Chapter 4

1. Jürgen Moltmann, *The Spirit of Life: A Universal Affirmation* (Minneapolis: Fortress, 1992), 233.

2. I am indebted to Jürgen Moltmann's preface to *The Trinity and the Kingdom* (1980; repr. Minneapolis: Fortress, 1991), xvi, for introducing me to Rublev's "Trinity" and to Henri Nouwen's reflection upon it in his *Behold the Beauty of the Lord: Praying with Icons* (Notre Dame, Ind.: Ave Maria Press, 1987), 19–27.

3. Matt. 20:23.

4. Karl Barth, *Church Dogmatics*, trans. G. W. Bromiley and T. F. Torrance (Edinburgh: T & T Clark, 1936–1969; New York: Scribner, 1955–1962), 1/1, 348. See Stanley J. Grenz and Roger E. Olson, *20th Century Theology: God & the World in a Transitional Age* (Downers Grove, Ill.: InterVarsity Press, 1992), 77: "One of Barth's greatest contributions to twentieth-century theology is his recovery of the doctrine of the Trinity from obscurity."

5. Dorothy L. Sayers, *Creed or Chaos?* (New York: Harcourt, Brace, 1949), 22.

6. See especially Miroslav Volf, *After Our Likeness: The Church as the Image of the Trinity* (Grand Rapids: Eerdmans, 1998).

7. Charles Partee, "Calvin's Central Dogma Again," *Sixteenth Century Journal* 18:2, 194. The focus of the *Institutes* "is not entirely [on] separate entities but on relationships."

8. Catherine Mowry LaCugna, *God for Us: The Trinity and Christian Life* (San Francisco: Harper and Row, 1991), 1, 22. See also Ted Peters, *GOD as Trinity: Relationality and Temporality in Divine Life* (Louisville: Westminster/John Knox, 1993), 7. For example, see Augustine, *On the Holy Trinity: A Select Library of the Nicene and Post-Nicene Fathers of the Christian Church*, edited by Philip Schaff (Buffalo: The Christian Literature Co., 1887), 9.

10. See John D. Zizoulas, *Being as Communion* (Crestwood, N.Y: St. Vladimir's Seminary Press, 1985). For a helpful analysis of Cappadocian thought, see Thomas Hopko, "The Trinity in the Cappadocians," in *Christian Spirituality: Origins to the Twelfth Century*, ed. B. McGinn and J. Meyendorff (New York: Crossroad, 1985), 260–75. A notable Western

exception and historical precedent is the twelfth-century writer Richard of St. Victor, *De Trinitate,* 3, 19, cited in Moltman, *Trinity and the Kingdom,* 19. For an introduction to Richard of St. Victor see Grover A. Zinn, trans. and introd. *Richard of St. Victor: the Twelve Patriarchs, the Mystical Ark, Book Three of the Trinity, in the Classics of Western Spirituality* (New York: Paulist, 1979) 3, 19. Most notable of these is Moltmann, *Trinity and the Kingdom,* 19.

11. While Barth posited a view of the Trinity *more* consistent with the psychological analogy of Augustine (where the *essence* of the Trinity is God's self-revelation of lordship), for Moltmann and other "social trinitarians," the *essence* or *substance* of God, that which is the divine unity, is nothing less than or other than the *communion of the Persons of the Godhead.* See Barth, *Church Dogmatics*, 1/1, 314. Cf. Moltmann, *Trinity and the Kingdom,* 177. Cf. *On the Holy Trinity,* 7.6.11. Augustine argues for an understanding of *essence* as the relationship between friends, relatives, or neighbors. The relationship of the Father and the Son can be expressed as the *essence* of their shared divinity.

12. Barth, *Church Dogmatics*, 1/1, 315.

13. Barth, *Church Dogmatics*, 1/1, 362.

14. William Placher, *Narratives of a Vulnerable God,* (Louisville: Westminster/John Knox, 1994), 73.

15. Placher, *Narratives,* 71. Cf. Augustine, *On the Holy Trinity*, 7.6.11: "For to God it is not one thing to be, another thing to be a person, but it is absolutely the same thing. For if the *to be* is said in respect to himself, but person relatively; in this way we should say three persons, the Father, Son and Holy Spirit just as we speak of three friends, or three relations, or three neighbors *in that they are so mutually, not that each one of them is so in respect to himself*" (emphasis mine).

16. Barth, *Church Dogmatics*, 1/1. For Volf (*After Our Likeness,* 204, 209), perichoresis helps us to understand and affirm each of the divine personae as a subject that is also mutually indwelling. "God's external works are not to be attributed to the one undifferentiated divine essence, but rather proceed from the divine persons." Yet, there is a "reciprocal interiority" of the trinitarian persons. "In every divine person as a subject, the other persons also indwell, all mutually permeate one another, though in doing so, they do not cease to be distinct persons."

17. Gregory of Nazianzus, *Theological Orations*, ed. and trans. E. R. Rochy, Library of Christian Classics 3 (Philadelphia: Westminster, 1960), 202.

18. Placher, *Narratives,* 73.

19. This maxim, popularly called "Rahner's Rule," is stated: "The 'economic' Trinity is the 'immanent' Trinity, and the 'immanent' Trinity is the 'economic' Trinity." See Karl Rahner, *The Trinity* (New York: Herder & Herder, 1970), 22. However, Christian theology has always affirmed that God is free *not* to be the same immanently as economically, because without that freedom, creation would be an act of necessity, not of freedom and grace. See also Placher (*Narratives,* 57–58), who reframes Rahner's Rule so that it avoids limiting God.

20. Thomas F. Torrance, *The Trinitarian Faith: The Evangelical Theology of the Ancient Catholic Church* (Edinburgh: T & T Clark, 1988), 52.

21. Bonhoeffer, *Sanctorum Communio* (London: Collins, 1957), 160.

22. Placher, *Narratives,* 73. See also Thomas F. Torrance, *The Mediation of Christ,* rev. ed. (Colorado Springs: Helmers & Howard, 1992), 110. Torrance says that we can understand God as Triune at all only through his actions in the atonement.

23. Zizoulas, *Being as Communion,* 16–17.

24. Zizoulas, *Being as Communion,* 17. See also Gregory of Nazianzus (*Theological Orations,* 171), who pointed out that "Father" is the name of a relation in which the Father

stands to the Son and the Son to the Father, not an *ousia* or *energeia*. Cf. Colin E. Gunton, *The Promise of Trinitarian Theology* (Edinburgh: T & T Clark, 1991), 72: "Communion is for Basil an ontological category. The *nature* of God is communion."

25. What theologians refer to as the "immanent" (who God is in himself) and "economic" (who God is revealed to be through his actions) Trinity.

26. Even though Moltmann disagrees with Barth on personhood in the Trinity, they agree on the same definition of human personhood. Moltmann, *Trinity and the Kingdom,* 17. Cf. Barth, *Church Dogmatics,* 1/1, 348.

27. Alistair I. McFadyen, *The Call to Personhood* (Cambridge: Cambridge University Press, 1990), 5. McFadyen cites Calvin, *Institutes,* 3.2.7, for a trinitarian definition of human faith: "A firm and certain knowledge of God's benevolence toward us, founded upon the truth of the freely given promise in Christ, both revealed to our minds and sealed upon our hearts through the Holy Spirit." See also, Volf, *After Our Likeness,* 182: "It is precisely the uniqueness of God's relation to me that makes me a unique human being."

28. Moltmann, *Trinity and the Kingdom,* 157.

29. Volf, *After Our Likeness,* 183.

30. Volf, *After Our Likeness,* 173.

31. "The perichoretic at-oneness of the Triune God corresponds to the experience of the community of Christ, the community which the Spirit unites through respect, affection and love" (Moltmann, *Trinity and the Kingdom,* 158).

32. LaCugna, *God for Us,* 228.

Chapter 5

1. See Colin E. Gunton, *The Promise of Trinitarian Theology* (Edinburgh: T & T Clark, 1991), 74.

2. William G. McLoughlin, *Revivals, Awakenings, and Reform: An Essay on Religion and Social Change in America, 1607–1977* (Chicago: University of Chicago Press, 1978), xiii.

3. 1 Cor. 5:5; 1 Tim. 1:18. Admittedly, this was a matter of church discipline that removed the believer from the fellowship, but the point is still the same. In the first century, to be outside of fellowship was considered a quite serious and even dangerous affair (vastly different than today).

4. Emil Brunner, *The Misunderstanding of the Church* (Philadelphia: Westminster, 1953), 12–13 (emphasis mine).

5. Jürgen Moltmann, *Trinity and the Kingdom* (1980; repr. Minneapolis: Fortress, 1991), 157.

6. Robert J. Banks, *Paul's Idea of Community: The Early House Churches in Their Social Setting* (Peabody, Mass.: Hendrickson, 1994), 26. See also Richard B. Hays, *The Moral Vision of the New Testament: Community, Cross, New Creation* (San Francisco: HarperCollins, 1996), 196. Hays asserts that from a New Testament perspective the central focus of spiritual and moral renewal is focused upon exhortations to the gathered community of disciples who live as a witness to an alternative vision of reality, and not primarily on individual renewal.

7. Brunner, *Misunderstanding of the Church,* 13. cf. 10. "The body of Christ is nothing other than the fellowship of persons," Brunner argues, in a critique of both "Protestant individualism and Catholic collectivism."

8. Jürgen Moltmann, *Spirit of Life: A Universal Affirmation* (Minneapolis: Fortress, 1992), 219. See also, Brunner, *Misunderstanding of the Church,* 11.

9. Placher, *Narratives,* 71.

10. Brunner, *Misunderstanding of the Church,* 12 (emphasis mine).

11. See Randy Frazee, *The Connecting Church* (Grand Rapids: Zondervan, 2001), 37. The author cites a speech by Lyle Schaller, who said, "The biggest challenge for the church opening the 21st century is to develop a solution to the discontinuity and fragmentation of the American lifestyle."

12. Miroslav Volf, *After Our Likeness: The Church as the Image of the Trinity* (Grand Rapids: Eerdmans, 1998), 207: "Ecclesial communion is always a communion of the will."

13. Barth, *Church Dogmatics*, 1/1, 241. "The proof of faith exists in the proclamation of faith."

14. Volf, *After Our Likeness,* 162 (emphasis mine).

15. Wayne A. Meeks, *The First Urban Christians: The Social World of the Apostle Paul* (New Haven: Yale University Press, 1984), 78.

16. Because many in Reformed circles naturally assume that "spiritual" is more closely related to "ethical," it is important to realize that Calvin generally thinks of God as personal, and of spirituality in relational categories. See Langdon Gilkey, *Reaping the Whirlwind: A Christian Interpretation of History* (New York: Seabury Press, 1976), 176. See also Calvin, *Inst.,* 3.6.3; and *Comm.* Eph. 5:29. Cf. C. Norman Kraus, *The Authentic Witness* (Grand Rapids: Eerdmans, 1979), 20.

17. Calvin, *Inst.* 4.14.18.

18. The Second Helvetic Confession, ch. xix.

19. Wallace describes Calvin's view of sacraments as God "taking up into his activity an earthly action or event and uniting with himself for a moment, a human element" (Ronald S. Wallace, *Calvin's Doctrine of the Word and Spirit* [Grand Rapids: Eerdmans, 1953], 159).

20. "For Calvin, as for Luther, there is no specific Eucharistic gift, no object, person, effect or grace given in the Eucharist which is not given in faith outside the Eucharist. . . . What Calvin says about our substantial union with Christ by reason of the Eucharist, can be said about our relationship with Christ quite apart from the Eucharist" (Killian McDonnell, *John Calvin, the Church and the Eucharist,* (Princeton: Princeton University Press, 1967), 179–180). B. A. Gerrish, *Grace and Gratitude: The Eucharistic Theology of John Calvin* (Minneapolis: Fortress, 1993), 158–59. Gerrish acknowledges that this reality has led to an unfortunate conflict between proponents of sacramental, as opposed to evangelical, piety, which has no basis in Calvin. It is precisely because the Spirit of God effects a union in the sacrament by faith that union with God is available outside the sacrament, too.

21. Donald M. Baillie, *The Theology of the Sacraments* (New York: Charles Scribner's Sons, 1957), 48–50.

22. Baillie, *Sacraments,* 47. "It is only when God speaks and awakens human faith that the natural object becomes sacramental. But this can happen to material things only because this is a sacramental universe, because God created all things visible and invisible."

23. Wolfhart Pannenberg, *Christian Spirituality* (Philadelphia: Westminster, 1983), 36, 38. "Since an effective symbol has been called a sacrament, I could speak of a sacramental, as well as a symbolic nature of the church."

24. See Robert J. Banks, *Going to Church in the First Century* (Beaumont: Christian Books, 1992), for a description of an early church gathering and celebration of the Lord's Supper.

25. Calvin, *Inst.* 4.1.9. Cf. Placher, *Narratives,* 137.

26. Calvin, *Inst.* 4.17.12. "The Lord bestows this benefit upon us through his Spirit so that we may be made one in body, spirit and soul with him. The bond of this connection is, therefore, the Spirit of Christ with whom we are joined in unity, and is like a channel through which all that Christ himself is and has conveyed to us." The section title is "Union with Christ as the Special Fruit of the Lord's Supper."

27. Baillie, *Theology of the Sacraments,* 54 (emphasis mine).

28. G. C. Berkouwer, *The Sacraments* (Grand Rapids: Eerdmans, 1969), 279. The Lord's Supper is an "act wherein is revealed the communion of believers with Christ and with each other."

29. Pannenberg, *Christian Spirituality,* 41. See also Gordon D. Fee, *The First Epistle to the Corinthians: New International Commentary on the New Testament* (Grand Rapids: Eerdmans, 1987), 557.

30. Fee, *First Epistle to the Corinthians,* 556.

31. Placher, *Narratives,* 146.

32. Berkouwer, *Sacraments*, 241, (emphasis mine). Cf. Wilhelm Niesel, "The Sacraments," in Donald K. McKim, ed. *Readings in Calvin's Theology* (Grand Rapids: Baker, 1984), 246. "In the Eucharist, his merciful condescension to the measure of our everyday realities attains its utmost extent."

Chapter 6

1. Ralph Martin, *Worship in the Early Church* (Grand Rapids: Eerdmans, 1964, rev. 1974), 10.

2. Though "building up the body" is a foundational component of worship as described in Eph. 4:12 and 1 Cor. 14:26.

3. *Contra* Randy Frazee, who has written that worship in a Christian community is specifically for the purpose of inspiring people to spiritual formation. See Frazee, *The Connecting Church* (Grand Rapids: Zondervan, 2001), 95–96: "Our goal is that when people walk out of the worship service each Sunday they will be inspired to suit-up for another exciting week of intentional faith-pursuit centered in Jesus Christ."

4. Indeed, the primary purpose of every person and everything (*including* spiritual formation) is to reveal and glorify God. According to James Torrance, that human purpose is to fulfill our task as the "priests of creation who express on behalf of all creation the praises of God." It is through wonder-filled human hearts and praising human lips that the "heavens declare the glory of God" with all creation serving as the "theatre of God's glory." See James B. Torrance, *Worship, Community & the Triune God of Grace* (Carlisle, U.K.: Paternoster, 1996), 1. This is, of course, the most memorable point made in the famous first question of the Westminster Shorter Catechism (1647–1648):

Q. What is the chief end of humanity?

A. The chief end of humanity is to glorify God and enjoy God forever.

Cf. Hughes Oliphant Old, *Worship That Is Reformed According to Scripture* (Atlanta: John Knox, 1984), 2: "We worship God because God created us to worship him. Worship is at the center of our existence, at the heart of our reason for being."

5. Charles Hodge, *The Classic New Testament Commentary: Ephesians,* ed. Philip Hillyer (London: Marshall Pickering, 1991), 28 (emphasis mine).

6. See Geoffrey Wainwright, *Doxology: The Praise of God in Worship, Doctrine and Life* (London: Epworth, 1980), 17. In the Letter to the Ephesians, the first chapter reveals that the people of God chosen "to the praise of his glorious grace" are to be "holy and blameless before [Christ] in love." Cf. Rom. 12:1–2; 2 Cor. 3:18.

7. Worship is work of the Holy Spirit, in the body of Christ, to the glory of the Father" (Old, *Worship That Is Reformed*), 8.

8. Walker Butin, "Reformed Ecclesiology: Trinitarian Grace according to Calvin," *Studies in Reformed Theology and History*, 2:1 (winter 1994), 19. "The trinitarian pattern which grounded the church's understanding of its existence and its communal life led in turn to [Calvin's] distinctive understanding of the church's worship, focused on *visibly enacting* the trinitarian grace of God" (emphasis mine). Cf. J. Torrance, *Worship, Community & the Triune God of Grace*, x: "The 'two horizons' of the Bible and our contemporary church life fuse in worship, as at the Lord's table, when we seek together, in a life of communion, to comprehend with the saints of all ages the Triune love of God in Christ."

9. It is an "ordinance of grace prescribed by God himself" (Robert Webber, *Worship Old & New: A Biblical, Historical, and Practical Introduction*, rev. ed. [Grand Rapids: Zondervan, 1994], 65). See also Robert Webber, *Signs of Wonder: The Phenomenon of Convergence in Modern Liturgical and Charismatic Churches* (Nashville: Abbott Martyn, 1992), 25, cited in Sally Morgenthaler, *Worship Evangelism* (Grand Rapids: Zondervan, 1995), 47.

10. Torrance, *Worship, Community*, 60.

11. Webber, *Worship Old & New*, 74.

12. Webber, *Worship Old & New*, 73.

13. Torrance, *Worship, Community*, 62.

14. James Hastings Nichols, *Corporate Worship in the Reformed Tradition* (Philadelphia: Westminster, 1968), 340.

15 Philip Walker Butin, *Revelation, Redemption, and Response: Calvin's Trinitarian Understanding of Divine-Human Relationship* (New York: Oxford University Press, 1995), 105.

16. James Hastings Nichols, *Corporate Worship in the Reformed Tradition* (Philadelphia: Westminster, 1968), 341.

Chapter 7

1. In Genesis 12, Abram is called by God to follow him, and at every stage of the journey Abram builds an altar to worship the God who "appeared to him." In Exod. 3: 18, and chapters 8 and 9, God appears to Moses and commissions him to declare to Pharaoh that God wants his people to worship him. The Decalogue begins in Exod. 20: 2–7 with God's declaration that his people must worship him alone, according to God's own prescriptions.

2. In the Psalms, calls to worship are not only the calls of the human worship leader, but God's own call to worship. The exhortation to sing a "new song" (Ps. 33:3, 96:1, 98: 1, 149:1) to the Lord is qualified by the affirmation that the Lord "put" a new song in the worshiper's mouth (Ps. 40:3).

3. Patrick Keifert, *Welcoming the Stranger: A Public Theology of Worship and Evangelism* (Minneapolis: Fortress, 1992), 58, 62.

4. In the New Testament the *ekklesia* is the local gathering where "the Lord is ever present with his people and governs them by his Spirit." See John Calvin, *Institutes* 4.8.11.

5. This whole section is a reiteration of the thesis of Kiefert, *Welcoming the Stranger.* This is an important and relatively neglected resource for the church's current discussions on worship (59–60).

6. See especially the calls to praise God among "the nations," e.g., Ps. 18:49, 45:17, 57:9, 106:47, 108:3, 117:1; Is. 66:19; 2 Sam. 22:50. Cf. Moses' clear instructions of how an "outsider" is admonished to act within Israel's worship in Numbers 15:14. Also, Paul's

use of the word *proskeneo* is only used to describe the unbeliever in the gathering who experiences the presence of God and falls down in worship.

7. Sally Morgenthaler, *Worship Evangelism* (Grand Rapids: Zondervan, 1995), 80–81; Kiefert, *Welcoming the Stranger,* 4.

8. Kennon L. Callahan, *Twelve Keys to an Effective Church: Strategic Planning for Mission* (San Francisco: Harper and Row, 1983), 23.

9. Kiefert, *Welcoming the Stranger,* 10.

10. Kiefert, *Welcoming the Stranger,* 8.

11. Gallup and Castelli, *The People's Religion,* 21. Gallup and Castelli describe the "Believers vs. Belongers" Gap in an American religious life: by virtually the same margin that personal religious belief increased in the last two decades, church membership and participation decreased. See also March 8, 1999, "Annual Survey of America's Faith Shows No Significant Changes in Past Year," from website www.barna.org.

12. What's more telling to me is that in an entire study of American religious life by Gallup and Castelli, there is not even one index reference to corporate sacraments.

13. Morgenthaler, *Worship Evangelism,* 49.

14. Furthermore, if the practical goal is a clearer understanding and heartfelt participation by a greater number of believers, then the church must continually note whom we exclude from being worship participants through our inadequate adaptation and education. Marva Dawn argues that one problem with contemporary worship that eschews liturgy or a traditional prayer is that children cannot learn the pieces ahead of time or read along in a worship bulletin. Not only children, but the disabled, the new believer, and the homebound can all be kept from full participation through a lack of proper attention and preparation, though I would add that Dawn underestimates how much more accessible to children are most praise choruses compared to traditional hymns. See Marva Dawn, *Reaching Out without Dumbing Down* (Grand Rapids: Eerdmans, 1995), 121.

15. While most larger churches tend to think of small groups as only part of fellowship or education and therefore disconnected from worship, I contend that the worship of the whole church should be aimed to be "completed" in the intimacy of a small group. With trained and commissioned lay people serving the sacraments under the oversight of the church leaders, small-group communion services are an excellent way to overcome some of the logistical roadblocks to more frequent celebrations of the Lord's Supper.

16. Hughes Oliphant Old, *Worship That Is Reformed According to Scripture* (Atlanta: John Knox, 1984), 74.

17. Indeed, Nichols has written that the Reformation was a "preaching revival" that is "probably the greatest in the history of the Church" (James Hastings Nichols, *Corporate Worship in the Reformed Tradition* [Philadelphia: Westminster, 1968], 29).

18. Morgenthaler, *Worship Evangelism,* 43.

19. Calvin, *Inst.* 4.1.5–6: "God himself appears in our midst, and as author by this order would have men recognize him as present in the institution." See also Nichols, *Corporate Worship,* 31: For the Reformers, "all that one could say about God's declaration and disclosure of himself in scripture is also true of his word preached."

20. Calvin, *Inst.* 4.1.5: "God breathes faith into us only by the instrument of his Gospel . . . [Rom 10:17]." Cf. Butin, *Revelation, Redemption, and Response,* 106. Butin draws attention to the intentional pneumatic wording of Calvin's interpretation of Rom. 10:7, stating, "Thus, [Calvin] makes explicit the trinitarian movement of this kind of preaching."

21. Gallup and Castelli, *People's Religion,* 90.

22. Gallup and Castelli, *People's Religion,* 21. The authors have identified three gaps in American Christianity: (1) the knowledge gap: the gap between a person's stated belief

and his or her knowledge of those beliefs; (2) the ethics gap: the gap between the degree of stated convictions and consistency in living them out; and (3) the "Believers vs. Belongers" gap: the gap between the rise in spiritual interest and the decrease in involvement with organized religion.

23. The Second Helvetic Confession, ch. 1.

24. See Kathryn Greene-McCreight, "What's the Story? The Doctrine of God in *Common Order* and the *Book of Common Worship,"* and Arlo D. Duba, "*The Book of Common Worship–The Book of Common Order:* What Do They Say and What Do They Assume about Christ?" both in Bryan D. Spinks and Iain D. Torrance, ed., *To Glorify God: Essays on Modern Reformed Liturgy* (Grand Rapids: Eerdmans, 1999),115–142.

25. James B. Torrance, *Worship, Community & the Triune God of Grace* (Carlisle, U.K.: Paternoster: 1996), 9.

26. If Scripture and sacrament is the clearest window through which to see God's own communion, then we must carefully consider not only *who* is included but also *how* we give the greatest visibility to God. Calvin's discussion of the Lord's Supper takes up this issue explicitly (Calvin, *Inst.* 4.17.23). It is precisely the "great pile of ceremonies," "spectacle," and "lifeless and theatrical trifles," that leads to a "people stupefied" and "dulled and befooled by superstition." Instead of creating a sense of awe in the presence of God, they hindered it. For Calvin, only this prohibited the sacrament from being served, as he wanted, every week—at least! Indeed, Calvin believed that all "who are in the least affected by piety" would "clearly see how much more brightly God's glory shines through" the simple ceremony of common bread and common wine.

27. A theme I will unpack more thoroughly in the next chapter; Calvin, *Inst.* 4.14.1. In defining sacraments, Calvin follows Augustine in calling them a "visible sign of a sacred thing." The sacraments are an "outward sign by which the Lord seals on our consciences the promises of his good will toward us in order to sustain our faith." Note the Lord is the actor in the sacrament. See also Butin, *Revelation, Redemption, and Response,* 106.

28. Calvin, *Inst.* 4.14.3.

29. Calvin, *Inst.* 4.17.43

30. The *Book of Order* of the PCUSA requires only quarterly Communion.

31. Karl Barth, *The Knowledge of God and the Service of God,* trans. J. L . M. Haire and Ian Henderson (London: Hodder and Stoughton, 1938), 211–12. Cited in Placher, *Narratives,* 156.

32. Gunton, *The Promise of Trinitarian Theology* (Edinburgh: T & T Clark, 1991), 72.

33. See Torrance (*Worship, Community,* 10–11), who writes, that the "supreme expression of all worship" from a trinitarian perspective is the Lord's Supper as an act in which the risen Lord meets us, helps us to recall his suffering love, and draws us into the shared communion of the Trinity.

34. Wolfhart Pannenberg, *Christian Spirituality* (Philadelphia: Westminster, 1983), 40.

35. Emil Brunner, *The Misunderstanding of the Church* (Philadelphia: Westminster, 1953), 67–68. According to Niesel, even "Calvin regards the church as essentially a Eucharistic fellowship. Wilhelm Niesel, "The Sacraments," in Donald K. McKim, ed. *Readings in Calvin's Theology* (Grand Rapids: Baker, 1984), 245.

36. See Calvin, *Inst.* 4.17.39: "The right administering of the sacrament cannot stand apart from the Word. For whatever benefit may come to us from the Supper requires the Word: whether we are confirmed in faith, or exercised in confession, or aroused to duty, there is need of preaching."

37. Even Bucer and Calvin, who championed preaching as the means of hearing from God directly, understood the Lord's Supper as the mystical union of the faithful with the "actually present risen Lord." Nichols, *Corporate Worship,* 45. For Calvin and Bucer, this "communion" is something "prior to and distinct from the appropriateness of his gifts of forgiveness."

38. Our denominational polity makes this more logistically problematic, but we are working to that end with our governing body.

39. Torrance, *Worship, Community,* 20, 87

40. Ralph P. Martin, *The Worship of God* (Grand Rapids: Eerdmans, 1982).

41. Martin, *Worship of God,* 19. Cf. Exod. 23:15–19; Deut. 18:4; Lev. 2:14; Prov. 3:9; Rev. 14:4–5, for just a few examples.

42. Nichols, *Corporate Worship*, 340: "The Reformers' concern that worship be in obedience to God was a concern to respect worship as an act of God. Worship that was not done in obedience to God was a mere work of human invention. . . . Worship that was done in obedience to God and through faith was an *act of God himself*" (emphasis mine).

43. Ronald S. Wallace, *Calvin's Doctrine of the Word and Spirit* (Grand Rapids: Eerdmans, 1953), 250. *Commentary* on John 4:22.

44. Calvin, cited in Wallace, *Calvin's Doctrine,* 251. Cf. *Comm.* John 6:15: "Modes of worship regulated to our fancy . . . have no other advantage than this that they rob God of his true honor and pour upon Him nothing but reproach."

45. Hughes Oliphant Old, "John Calvin and the Prophetic Criticism of Worship," in *John Calvin and the Church: A Prism of Reform,* ed. Timothy George (Louisville: Westminster/John Knox, 1990), 233.

46. Cf. Old, "John Calvin and the Prophetic Criticism," 231.

47. Nichols, *Corporate Worship,* 12–18.

48. Old, *Worship That Is Reformed,* 48.

49. Calvin, *Inst.* 3.20.32. Cf. Nichols, *Corporate Worship,* 32.

Chapter 8

1. Dallas Willard, "Spiritual Formation in Christ: A Perspective on What It Is and How It Might Be Done," given at Fuller Theological Seminary, October 22, 1993. Ironically, this is the same indictment of theological liberalism by the "postliberals" like Stanley Hauerwas (*A Community of Character: Toward a Constructive Christian Social Ethic* [Notre Dame, Ind.: University of Notre Dame Press, 1981]) and George Lindbeck (*The Nature of Doctrine: Religion and Theology in a Postliberal Age* [Philadelphia: Westminster, 1984]).

2. See, for example, Louis Berkhof, *Systematic Theology* (Grand Rapids: Eerdmans, orig. publ. 1939, reprinted, 1991), 543: The Spirit of God is the "Spirit of obedience, so that without any constraint [the believer] willingly obeys the law."

3. For the Reformed Christians of my own theological tradition, this is particularly worrisome. We boldly declare that we are "Reformed, always reforming, by the Word of God." The original motto, *ecclesia reformata, semper reformanda,* is attributed to Dutch theologian Gisbert Voetius (1588–1676) a strict high-Calvinist who was part of the Synod of Dort and opposed the then highly popular Cartesian philosophy as being too subjective and not reliant enough upon the Scriptures. As Harold Nebelsick notes, "Voetius was convinced that the life of the church and its members was to be reformed continually by the scriptural Word of God. Both the members of the church and the church itself were to bow ever again before that Word. They were to repent and in repenting they were to take with utter seriousness the words, 'Be ye Holy as I am Holy.' They were to be set

apart from the world and to reflect the very life of the Church in the World." (See Harold Nebelsick, "Ecclesia Reformata Semper Reformanda," *Reformed Liturgy and Music,* 18: 2 [spring 1984], reprinted in *Exploring Presbyterian Worship* [Louisville: Christian Faith and Life Congregation Ministries Division, 1994], 4.) This oft-repeated statement, which is used primarily to define and guide doctrinal and ecclesiastical change, is also relevant to individual transformation. Donald McKim, in his introduction to *Major Themes of the Reformed Tradition* (Grand Rapids: Eerdmans, 1992), xiv, described the Swiss Reformers of the sixteenth century as those whose "comprehensive commitment and underlying foundation" was to "reform all life according to the Word of God." This thought is also picked up in the preface to the most recent confessional document of the Presbyterian Church (U.S.A.), *A Brief Statement of Faith,* published in the *Book of Confessions* (Louisville: Office of the General Assembly of the PCUSA), where it states, "From the first, the Reformed churches have insisted that the renewal of the church must become visible in the transformation of human lives and societies."

4. As will be clear, I do not in any way wish to diminish the authoritative foundation and formative function of the Scripture in the evangelical tradition (quite the opposite!). I simply mean to frame the discussion about the use of Scripture, not around the usual loci of authority and interpretation, but instead around the practical concerns of how Scripture inspires faith and forms disciples.

5. See Timothy R. Phillips and Dennis L. Okholm, eds., *The Nature of Confession: Evangelicals and Postliberals in Conversation* (Downers Grove, Ill.: InterVarsity Press, 1996). Recent conversations across the theological spectrum have demonstrated that ironically, both conservative evangelicals and liberals use a modernist paradigm for biblical authority and interpretation—with similar unfortunate results. As Phillips and Okholm have written, "modern theories of biblical interpretation find the meaning of the text in something more basic and foundational than scripture—a universally accessible reality. Whether meaning was found in eternal truths that the text symbolized (for liberals) or identified exclusively with the story's factual reference (as for conservatives), both displaced the priority of scripture. . . . When another authority was found, scripture's world-forming narrative was fragmented and eventually dispersed. This shift in understanding—the loss of scripture's grand narrative as well as its christological center and unity—impeded the biblical narrative from shaping the Community of disciples" (11; emphasis mine). It is exactly that "shaping of the Community of disciples" that is most lacking and in need of addressing.

6. See Karl Barth, *Church Dogmatics*, 1/1, 4, who defines the Word as the Word Revealed in Jesus Christ, the Word Preached and the Word written. See also Otto Weber (*Foundations of Dogmatics*, trans. D. Guder [Grand Rapids: Eerdmans, 1982]), who uses a similar motif to talk of the Word as Event in Jesus Christ, the Word Witnessed To in Scripture, and the Proclaimed Word of preaching.

7. John 1:17; 2 Cor. 4:6. See also The Theological Declaration of Barmen, published in the *Book of Confessions* (Louisville: Office of the General Assembly of the PCUSA, 1997), 8.11:"Jesus Christ as he is attested for us in Holy Scripture, is the one Word of God which we have to hear and which we have to trust and obey in life and in death."

8. Gabriel Fackre, "Narrative: Evangelical, Postliberal, Ecumenical," in *The Nature of Confession,* ed. Timothy R. Phillips and Dennis L. Okholm (Downers Grove, Ill.: InterVarsity Press, 1996), 126. "One of the signs of . . . the priorities with [the] canonical process itself [is that] the church lifts above itself the biblical canon, thereby declaring its accountability to scripture." Barth warns that this should best be understood, not as *inspiration,* but *inspiredness.* For Barth, the Scriptures are inspired by the voice of God

in Jesus as a free gift of grace and can be accessed only indirectly, by faith. Barth views "verbal inspiration" as a "product of typical rationalistic thinking," which seeks to separate the inspired Scriptures from the "inspiring" God. In other words, only through the life of the Spirit and faith in God do the Scriptures reveal God. No "objective" standard of "secular experience" would lead to this conclusion. See Barth, *Church Dogmatics,* 4/1, 368, cited in Klaas Runia, *Karl Barth's Doctrine of Holy Scripture* (Grand Rapids: Eerdmans, 1962), 118.

9. The Second Helvetic Confession, published in the *Book of Confessions,* 5.001: "We believe and confess the canonical scriptures . . . to be the true Word of God. . . . For God himself . . . speaks to us through Holy scripture" (1 Thess. 2:13, Matt. 10:26, and parallels). The Westminster Catechisms and Confession of Faith, published in the *Book of Confessions* (Louisville: Office of the General Assembly of the PCUSA, 1997), 7.002, 7.113, 7.114

10. The Second Helvetic Confession, 5.004: "The preaching of the Word of God is the Word of God."

11. Nicholas Lash, *Theology on the Way to Emmaus* (London: SCM, 1986), 42. See also David Scott, "Speaking to Form: Trinitarian-Performative Scripture Reading," in *Anglican Theological Review* 77:2 (spring 1995), 137–159. See also Stephen Barton, "New Testament Interpretation as Performance," *Scottish Journal of Theology,* 52:2 (1999), 195. As Barton demonstrates, a performance approach to Scripture is laudable because it "goes *with* the grain both of the NT itself and of the Bible as a whole" where it "invites completion in the lives of its readers." See also Stephen E. Fowls and L. Gregory Jones, *Reading in Communion: Scripture and Ethics in Christian Life* (Grand Rapids: Eerdmans, 1991), 20: "Christian communities interpret scripture, then, so that believers might live faithfully before God in the light of Jesus Christ. The aim of faithful living before the Triune God must become the standard to which all interpretive interests must measure up."

12. This is similar to Walter Wink's exhortation to "whole-brained exegesis," where "left-brained analysis and criticism" is integrated into a "right-brained" affective and evocative interaction with the biblical text so as to challenge our own self-centered and culturally affirmed assumptions and instead to live out an "encounter with the text by the total self" (Walter Wink, *Transforming Bible Study,* 2d ed. [Nashville: Abingdon, 1989), 28–31. Cf. Fowl and Jones, *Reading in Communion,* 29: "The interpretation of scripture . . . involves a life-long process of learning to become a wise reader of the scripture capable of embodying that reading in life."

13. Augustine, *The Confessions of Saint Augustine* (Oak Harbor, Wash.: Logos Research Systems, 1995).

14. Ronald S. Wallace, *Calvin's Doctrine of the Word and Spirit* (Grand Rapids: Eerdmans, 1953), 7, Cf. Calvin, *Comm.* Gen. 32:30: in the gospel, Christ, "the living image of God, is evidently set before our eyes."

15. John Leith, "Calvin's Doctrine of the Proclamation of the Word and Its Significance Today," in *John Calvin and the Church: A Prism of Reform,* ed. Timothy George (Louisville: Westminster/John Knox, 1990), 209, 211. "Calvin . . . was so sure that in preaching, God himself is present. . . . [He] understood preaching to be a sacrament of the saving presence of God . . . something of a divine epiphany."

16. See Calvin's *Comm.* 1 Cor. 13:12: "The ministry of the Word, I say is like a looking glass." Cited in Wallace, *Calvin's Doctrine,* 24.

17. From the introduction to his essay "The Meaning and Content of the Icon," which was adapted from Leonid Ouspensky, *Theology of the Icon,* trans. Anthony Gythiel and Elizabeth Meyendorff, 2 vols. (Crestwood, N.Y.: St. Vladimir's Seminary Press, 1992), 1:

151–94, and printed in *Eastern Orthodox Theology: A Contemporary Reader*, ed. Daniel B. Clendenin (Grand Rapids: Baker, 1995), 33–63.

18. Ouspensky, "Meaning and Content of the Icon," 35.

19. Ouspensky, "Meaning and Content of the Icon," footnote, 46.

20. Calvin, *Comm.* Haggai 1:12, cited in Wallace, *Calvin's Doctrine,* 82. Cf. John 1:14–18.

21. Calvin, *Inst.* 4.14.26: "Words are nothing else but signs."

22. See Calvin's *Comm.* 1 Cor. 13:12, cited in Wallace, *Calvin's Doctrine,* 24.

23. The Second Helvetic Confession, ch. 1, 5.004.

24. For example, see Robert Guelich, *The Sermon on the Mount: A Foundation for Understanding* (Dallas: Word, 1982), 67. Guelich says that the Beatitudes are declaratory statements that, like the ministerial statement "I now pronounce you husband and wife," create the very effect they announce. This is also the effect of Jesus' preaching of the Gospel in Mark 1:14–15 and parallels. To hear that the "Kingdom of God is at hand" is to hear the "good news."

25. Wallace, *Calvin's Doctrine,* 7. Calvin taught that throughout salvation-history God is always "veiling himself in order to reveal himself." In the Reformed tradition, the bread, wine, and words are themselves a sign, window, or icon to a reality beyond themselves as the presence of Christ by the Holy Spirit.

26. See especially Calvin, *Inst.* 3.1.1, 3.2.24, 4.17.3.

27. Calvin, *Inst.* 4.14.8.

28. Peter Toon, *Our Triune God: A Biblical Portrayal of the Trinity* (Wheaton, Ill.: Victor, 1996), 62.

29. Gabriel Fackre, *The Christian Story,* rev. ed. (Grand Rapids: Eerdmans, 1984), 4.

30. See N. T. Wright, *The New Testament and the People of God* (Minneapolis: Fortress, 1992), 372 (emphasis in original). See also Miroslav Volf, "Theology, Meaning and Power: A Conversation with George Lindbeck on Theology & the Nature of Christian Difference," in *The Nature of Confession,* 59: "Because Christian faith is not a philosophy resting on a principle, but a religion involving a drama (God's complex history with the world he created), narrative is the most basic way to talk about faith." Cf. Stanley Hauerwas, *A Community of Character,* 10: "The Church is a people on a journey who insist on living consistently the conviction that God is the Lord of history."

31. As in 1 Peter 2:9–10, where a mostly Gentile audience is addressed in these Old Testament terms: "But you are a chosen race, a royal priesthood, a holy nation, God's own people, in order that you may proclaim the mighty acts of him who called you out of darkness into his marvelous light. Once you were not a people, but now you are God's people; once you had not received mercy, but now you have received mercy."

32. Fackre, *Christian Story,* 7–10. Narrative theology has three "distinct but overlapping forms": the "canonical story" of biblical materials, the "life story" of human experience, and the "community story" of classical Christian tradition. While there could be some debate about which form gets priority of place, the narrative, to be spiritually formative, "take[s] its shape from biblical faith." Fackre (9–10), who writes from the perspective of community story, insists that narrative theology attend not only to text and experience, but also "vis-à-vis the orientation points of the historic faith." By doing so, it then eschews both the "heartless propositionalism" (seen in extreme conservatism) and the "mindless imagination" (seen in some extreme liberalism), while bringing together the "power of the text, the drama of life experience, and the lore of the Christian Community."

33. N. T. Wright, *New Testament and the People of God,* 77. See also George Stroup, *The Promise of Narrative Theology: Recovering the Gospel in the Church* (Atlanta: John Knox,

1981), 254: "Revelation occurs as the Christian narrative collides with personal identity and the latter is reconstructed by the former."

34. Gabriel Fackre, "Narrative Theology: An overview," *Interpretation* 37, October 1983, 345.

35. George W. Stroup, "Narrative in Calvin's Hermeneutic," in *John Calvin and the Church: A Prism of Reform* ed. Timothy George (Louisville: Westminster/John Knox, 1990), 163.

36. Eric Auerbach, *Mimesis,* trans. Willard R. Trask (Princeton: Princeton University Press, 1953), 15; cited by George Stroup, "Narrative in Calvin's Hermeneutic," 163.

37. Hauerwas, *Community of Character,* 52: "The social ethical task of the church is to be the kind of Community that tells and tells rightly the story of Jesus. . . . We, like the early Christians, must learn that understanding Jesus' life is inseparable from learning how to live our own."

38. Fackre, "Narrative," in *Nature of Confession,* 127–28.

39. Volf, "Theology, Meaning and Power," 57. It seems beyond doubt that one becomes a human being not only by learning one's mother's language but also by feeling her touch and hearing the sound of her voice. Similarly, we become Christians not only by learning the language of faith but also by being "touched" by other Christians and ultimately by God on a nonsemiotic level. The Christian semiotic system lives in the lives of the people of God through the interplay of nonsemiotic dimensions of church life (which are meaningless without the semiotic) and semiotic dimensions of church life (which are powerless without the nonsemiotic.

40. Wright, *New Testament and the People of God,* 448–49.

41. Cf. J. Leith, "Calvin's Doctrine of the Proclamation of the Word and Its Significance for Today," in *John Calvin and the Church: A Prism of Reform,* ed. Timothy George (Louisville: Westminster/John Knox, 1990), 215. Leith writes that for Calvin "preaching is not only the *explication* of scripture, but the *application* of scripture. Just as Calvin explicated the scriptures word-by-word, so he applied the scripture sentence by sentence to the life and experience of his congregation."

42. Stanley Hauerwas, "Casuistry as a Narrative Art," *Interpretation* 37, October 1983, 379. The direct prohibitions or imperatives of a community help one to specifically lead "one's life in terms of the narrative that forms the Community's understanding of its basic purpose."

43. Hauerwas, "Casuistry as a Narrative Art," 380. However, this does not mean that traditional prescriptions are always heeded without any moral deliberation. Hauerwas also sees moments of "moral crises" as a test for the community to determine whether it has accurately interpreted its narrative and the "practical force of its conviction."

44. Calvin, *Comm.* Ps. 106:39, cited in Wallace, *Calvin's Doctrine,* 99.

45. Calvin, *Inst.* 2.7.12.

46. The Heidelberg Catechism, Q. 1.

47. The Heidelberg Catechism, Q. 115.

48. Calvin, *Inst.* 4.8.6.

Chapter 9

1. In 1998 we organized our entire congregation in "neighborhood parishes" of fifteen to twenty families, with trained leaders serving each neighborhood. As our church has grown larger, these parishes help us stay "small."

2. Gordon Fee, *God's Empowering Presence: The Holy Spirit in the Letters of Paul* (Peabody, Mass.: Hendrickson, 1994), 319: "Indeed, through Christ and by the Spirit we are being transformed so as to bear the likeness for which we were intended at the beginning. In the freedom the Spirit provides, we have seen the glory of God himself—as it is made evident to us in the face of our Lord Jesus Christ—and we have come to experience that glory, and will do so in an ever increasing way until we come to the final glory. . . . *By the Spirit we not only come to know God, but come to live in his Presence in such a way as constantly to be renewed in God's image*" (emphasis mine).

3. Calvin, *Comm.* 1 Cor. 13:12. See also Wallace, *Calvin's Doctrine of Word and Sacrament*, 24–26: "The same self-revealing Lord who shows himself to the people of Israel and in many and varied forms, ceremonies, dreams and visions, confronts us today when the Word is preached and the sacraments administered, and it is to the Word and sacraments that we must turn if we wish to enter into communion with him." Cf. Calvin, *Comm.* Gen. 28:17: "The preaching of the Gospel is called the Kingdom of heaven and the sacraments may be called the gate of heaven, because they admit us into the presence of God."

4. Nicholas Lash, *Theology on the Way to Emmaus* (London: SCM, 1986), 46.

5. According to Augustinian tradition, the *verbum visible* (Richard Muller, *Dictionary of Latin and Greek Theological Terms* [Grand Rapids: Baker, 1985], 325), and according to Emil Brunner, *verbum communale* and *verbum activum* (Brunner, *The Misunderstanding of the Church* [Philadelphia: Westminster, 1953], 68).

6. Calvin, *Institutes* 4.17.3

7. Ronald S. Wallace, *Calvin's Doctrine of the Word and Spirit* (Grand Rapids: Eerdmans, 1953), 240–41. According to Wallace, Calvin attributed to the sacraments the ability to "unite us more fully with Christ," to "confirm and increase the faith of believers" as a "continual support" and as a "spur to practical Christian living."

8. Calvin, *Inst.* 4.17.38.

9. Robert J. Banks, "Home Churches and Spirituality," *Interchange* 40 (1986), 16.

10. George Stroup, "Narrative in Calvin's Hermeneutic," 158.

11. Richard B. Hays, *The Moral Vision of the New Testament: Community, Cross, New Creation* (San Francisco: HarperCollins, 1996), 196.

12. Henry H. Knight III, "True Affections: Biblical Narrative & Evangelical Spirituality" in Phillips and Okholm, eds., *The Nature of Confession*, 198 (emphasis mine). Knight asserts that evangelical theology need not ever be insulated from spirituality, because its spirituality "is formed within a Community whose life is shaped by the biblical narrative."

13. Jonathan L. Wilson, "Toward a New Evangelical Paradigm of Biblical Authority," in Phillips and Okholm, eds., *The Nature of Confession*, 157.

14. See Stanley Grenz, *Theology for the Community of God* (Nashville: Broadman and Hollman, 1994), 495: "The Bible is the Spirit's book, its purpose is instrumental to his mission." Cf. Muller, *Dictionary of Latin and Greek Theological Terms*, 324. In traditional Reformed sources, the church *follows* the scriptures as *ecclesia nata est ex Dei Verbo* ("The church is born of the Word of God"). "In historical fact, there has always been a people of God before the written Word . . . but the concept of an unwritten Word . . . that constitutes both the call of the people and the basis of the written Word argues for the priority of Word over church. The concept also takes into account the centuries recounted in Genesis before any written scripture, during which the Word of God called and led the people of God." See also Wolfhart Pannenberg, *Christian*

Spirituality (Philadelphia: Westminster, 1983), 40; and Brunner, *Misunderstanding of the Church*, 11.

15. For an insightful critique of the formal lectionary, see David G. Buttrick, "Preaching the Lectionary: Two Cheers and Some Questions," in *Reformed Liturgy and Music* 28: 2 (spring 1994), 77–81.

16. Irvine (California) Presbyterian Church developed a two-year program for reading the entire Bible together. Bookmarks with the monthly reading assignments were made available for any who wanted to take part.

17. See James W. McClendon Jr., *Systematic Theology: Ethics* (Nashville: Abingdon, 1986), 33.

18. Curtis Freeman, "Toward a *Sensus Fidelium* for an Evangelical Church," 169. See also David Scott, "Speaking to Form: Trinitarian-Performative Scripture Reading," in *Anglican Theological Review* 77:2 (spring 1995), 137–159," 143.

19. Walter Brueggemann asserts that the Scriptures provide the elements of (or "fund") an imagined world that is counter to the secular constructs we live in. This imaginative act is a response to God where we consider the world not as it is, but as God intends it, and covenant to live accordingly. See Walter Brueggemann, *Texts under Negotiation: The Bible and Postmodern Imagination* (Philadelphia: Fortress, 1993).

20. For a fine description and discussion of *lectio divina,* see Norvene Vest, *Bible Reading for Spiritual Growth* (San Francisco: HarperCollins, 1993); or M. Robert Mulholland, *Invitation to a Journey* (Downers Grove, Ill.: InterVarsity Press, 1993), 112–15.

21. Leonid Ouspensky, "The Meaning and Content of the Icon," in *Theology of the Icon*, trans. Anthony Gythiel and Elizabeth Meyendorff, 2 vols. (Crestwood, N.Y.: St. Vladimir's Seminary Press, 1992), 59.

Chapter 10

1. Richard B. Hays, *The Moral Vision of the New Testament: Community, Cross, New Creation* (San Francisco: HarperCollins, 1996), 196 (emphasis mine).

2. C. S. Lewis, *The Screwtape Letters* (1942; repr. San Francisco: HarperCollins, 2001), 12.

3. Prayer as it is understood here is personal self-identification with all of humanity and a participation in the work of the reign of God. See Karl Barth, *Prayer,* ed. Don Saliers (1949; repr. Philadelphia: Westminster, 1985), 25. See also Donald Bloesch, *The Struggle of Prayer*, Colorado Springs, Col.: Helmers & Howard, 1988), 158.

4. For an excellent and detailed analysis of this prayer, see George R. Beasley-Murray, *Word Biblical Commentary,* vol. 36: *John* (Waco, Tex.: Word, 1987).

5. Beasley-Murray, *Word Biblical Commentary*, 293 (emphasis mine).

6. Beasley-Murray, *Word Biblical Commentary,* 294: "Jesus prays that the disciples will be 'kept faithful in a hostile world, that they may share in the consecration of Jesus for the salvation of the world, that they may be one in Christ, that the world may see the love of the Lord embodied in them, that they at the last may behold the glory of Jesus in the company of the Father and share in it.'"

7. Beasley-Murray points out that the wording of verse 19, "for their sakes ("on their behalf," "ὑπὲρ αὐτῶν"), is similar to the communion language of the Lord's Supper and, therefore, "must surely indicate an overlap in the meaning of consecration of Jesus and that of his disciples; his dedication unto death is made in order that they too may be dedicated to the same task of bringing the saving sovereignty into the world *in like spirit as he brought it* . . . this they will best do as they exemplify the suffering love of the Redeemer" (Beasley-Murray, *Word Biblical Commentary,* 301 [emphasis in original]).

8. Beasley-Murray, following E. C. Hoskyns, sees the focal point of the passage in verse 19: *"And for their sakes I sanctify myself, so that they also may be sanctified in truth."*

9. John 17 uses the word *glorify* for what I am calling *witness.* I am emphasizing the sense by which being a witness to God is to reveal, reflect, and make visible the presence of God.

10. Beasley-Murray, *Word Biblical Commentary,* 293. Beasley-Murray follows most commentators in seeing John 17 as instruction in the form of a prayer.

11. As we examine this prayer we also see that, for Jesus, the disciples' effectiveness in witnessing to God's presence is dependent on God's own activity. (See Karl Barth, *Evangelical Theology: An Introduction*, trans. Grover Foley [1963; repr. Grand Rapids: Eerdmans, 1986], 160). They need to be "kept" (John 17:11b, a better translation than the NRSV "protected") in the "name of God," a reference to loyalty to God and adherence to the character of God revealed in Jesus. (This phrase anticipates v. 17, where the disciples are sanctified "in the truth, your word is truth.") See also Beasley-Murray, *Word Biblical Commentary,* 298–99. Thus, for Jesus, faithfulness to God precedes unity, and unity is dependent upon the revelation of God in Jesus.

12. Beasley-Murray, *Word Biblical Commentary,* 306. See also G. K. Barrett, *John*, 512: "The Father sends the Son and in his works the love of the Father for mankind is manifest, because the Son lives always in the unity of love with the Father; the Son sends the church, and in the mutual charity and humility which exists within the unity of the church the life of the Son and the Father is reflected."

13. Barth, *Prayer,* 41.

14. See Rodney Clapp, "Remonking the Church: Would a Protestant Form of Monasticism Help Liberate Evangelicalism from Its Cultural Captivity?" in *Christianity Today,* August 12, 1988, 20–21. Clapp suggests that an evangelical "remonasticism" would be committed to in-depth Scripture study and faithful performance and a life of prayer that will model to the greater church the possibilities for spiritual growth.

15. Martin Thornton, *Pastoral Theology: A Reorientation* (London: SCPK, 1956), 24.

16. Beasley-Murray, *Word Biblical Commentary,* 294.

17. Simon Chan, *Spiritual Theology: A Systematic Study of the Christian Life* (Downers Grove, Ill.: InterVarsity Press, 1998), 105.

18. For two widely read examples, see Stanley Hauerwas and William H. Willimon, *Resident Aliens* (Nashville: Abingdon, 1989); and Rodney Clapp, *Peculiar People: The Church as Culture in a Post-modern Society* (Downers Grove, Ill.: InterVarsity Press, 1996).

19. Chan, *Spiritual Theology,* 105–06.

20. Thornton, *Pastoral Theology,* 22–25.

21. Martin Thornton, *Christian Proficiency* (1959; repr. Cambridge, Mass.: Cowley, 1988). See chapter 5 on "rule" as an expression of a "regular" disciplined time of prayer and chapter 6 on "recollection as the "habit of tuning to God at regular times during the workday." See also Chan, *Spiritual Theology,* 137–38.

22. Biblically, the "remnant" people of God are those who are chosen and saved from destruction as a sign of God's faithfulness. While both Thornton and Chan oppose seeing the remnant as superior to or better than the regular congregation of the church (indeed, they describe the remnant as those with a "call" or "vocation" to encourage spiritual vitality in the whole body), remnant language implies judgment on the non-remnant. See the article on *leimma* in Gerhard Kittel and Gerhard Friedrich, eds., *The Theological Dictionary of the New Testament,* trans. and abr. George W. Bromiley (Grand Rapids: Eerdmans, 1985).

23. I am using the term "sanctify themselves" as a way of connecting to John 17:19, where Jesus refers to his faithful action as "consecrating" or "sanctifying" himself *and* the disciples.

24. Darrell L. Guder et. al, eds., *Missional Church* (Grand Rapids: Eerdmans, 1998), 105.

25. See Thornton, *Christian Proficiency,* chapters 5 and 6, for the description of just such a rule.

26. For discussion on John 17 as part of the Last Supper discourse of John 13–17, see Beasley-Murray, *Word Biblical Commentary,* 295–96.

27. Robert J. Banks, *Paul's Idea of Community: The Early House Churches in Their Social Setting* (Peabody, Mass.: Hendrickson, 1994), 85.

28. 1 Cor. 11:26. Cf. Banks, *Paul's Idea of Community,* 84: "The meal itself was a visible proclamation of the death of Christ to all who participated in it, and therefore, a call to discipleship by him."

29. Bloesch reminds us that all prayer in a "prophetic religion" that speaks to the world is "not solitary contemplation . . . but instead blessed fellowship, the 'beloved community.' Solitary prayer is still important, but it is a secondary goal. Our attention should be focused not so much on the vision of God as the service of God. Our aim is to glorify God in the worship of him and the service of our neighbor." Bloesch, *The Struggle of Prayer,* 165.

30. See Banks, *Paul's Idea of Community,* 81–84. Banks, who greatly emphasizes the meal as a reminder of believers' fellowship with Christ and each other, and sees no cultic significance in Paul's instruction on the meal, characterizes the main distinction between Paul's understanding of the Lord's Supper and the mystery cult feasts of the Roman paganism as the centrality of the Christian meal as an "occasion for mutual fellowship and service."

31. Banks, *Paul's Idea of Community,* 82.

32. Bloesch, *Struggle of Prayer,* 165. "The Christian faith is not only deeply personal but also radically social. Its concern is not just with the salvation of individual souls but with the holy community." Cf. p. 167: "The final goal of prayer is both personal salvation and the transformation of the world."

Chapter 11

1. The classic text in this regard is Ignatius of Loyola's *Spiritual Exercises.* See Ignatius of Loyola, *Spiritual Exercises and Selected Texts,* ed. George E. Ganss, S. J. (New York: Paulist, 1991). Some contemporary works include Thomas H. Green, S. J., *Weeds among the Wheat: Discernment, Where Prayer & Action Meet* (Notre Dame, Ind.: Ave Maria Press, 1984), and Danny E. Morris and Charles M. Olsen, *Discerning God's Will Together: A Spiritual Practice for the Church* (Nashville: Upper Room, 1997).

2. See Luke Timothy Johnson, *Scripture and Discernment: Decision Making in the Church* (1983; repr. Nashville: Abingdon, 1996), 112. According to Johnson, in the New Testament, Paul "most explicitly and extensively speaks of discernment and most emphatically placed it at the heart of the Christian *moral* life" (emphasis mine).

3. Richard B. Hays, *The Moral Vision of the New Testament: Community, Cross, New Creation* (San Francisco: HarperCollins, 1996), 197: "The coherence of the New Testament's ethical mandate will come into focus only when we understand that mandate in *ecclesial* terms, when we seek God's will not by asking 'What should I do' but 'What should we do?'"

4. James D. G. Dunn, "Discernment of Spirits—A Neglected Gift," in *Witness to the Spirit: Essays on Revelation, Spirit, and Redemption,* ed. Wilfrid Harrington (Dublin: Irish

Biblical Association, 1979), 714. According to Dunn, Romans 12:1–2 refers to something more "charismatically immediate than formal," defined by Oscar Cullman as "a capacity of forming correct Christian *ethical* judgment at each given moment" (emphasis mine). But, one may ask, what about those narratives that seem to describe a process of specific decision making in the early church? Don't those demonstrate a method for determining "God's will" in a given situation? Let us consider two examples. First, in Acts 1:20–26, the Apostles faced the decision of replacing Judas with one of the large number of followers. Second, in Acts 6:1–7, the early community chose seven Greek-speaking believers to minister alongside the Twelve. In each case, the community set out a criterion based on character qualities and experience, prayed, and came to a decision that was embraced by the whole community. While Johnson *(Scripture and Discernment)* emphasizes prayer (Acts 1:14) and discernment, there is no mention of a "method." The community was devoted to prayer, the Apostles decided upon some qualifications, and then decisions were made that all the people approved. The emphasis of the texts is the prayerful community making decisions based on agreed-upon criteria, with consensus of the whole. Drawing upon several passages in Acts, Luke Timothy Johnson posits a method of discernment based upon the telling of narratives by trusted individuals with reference to Scripture. Referring to Acts 4:23–31, Johnson (*Scripture and Discernment,* 84) writes that the leaders establish a pattern of narrating and praying. Cf. Johnson, *Scripture and Discernment,* 88, where referring to Acts 9:26–30, Johnson demonstrates that narrations depend upon the character of the narrator. The church, in large part, accepts Paul because Barnabas was a "trusted member." For Johnson, the power of the narrative, spoken in the community by "trusted members," prayerfully considered, and accurately connected to the scriptural tradition, offers evidence of the Spirit's work.

5. In addition to δοκιμάζω, the Greek words most commonly translated as "discern," "determine," or "test" are διακρίσεις, mostly found in 1 Cor. 12: 8–10 and 1 Cor. 14:29, and ἀνακρίνω, found in 1 Cor 2:14–16. In 1 Cor. 12–14, Paul is addressing issues related to what it means to be a spiritual person. In 12:10 and 14:29 the same verb refers to the "distinguishing" or "weighing" of prophecies or other "spiritual utterances." Paul's intent is to encourage the Corinthians' zeal for "manifestations of the Spirit" (v. 7), toward edification of the body. (Cf. 1 Cor. 14:12: "So with yourselves; since you are eager for spiritual gifts, strive to excel in them for building up the church.") While the Corinthians tended to view those with ecstatic experiences as the most spiritually mature, for Paul, the hallmark of spiritual maturity was always and consistently *faithful confession* and *communal edification*. (See Fee, *First Epistle to the Corinthians*, 570, 585. Cf. 1 Cor. 14:5: "so that the church will be built up.") As Gordon Fee explains (*First Epistle to the Corinthians*, 573), "they must cultivate loving, personal relationships in the body of Christ; and their times of public worship must be for mutual edification, not heightened individualistic spirituality, which in their case had become a false spirituality." Eduard Schweizer ("What Is the Holy Spirit? A Study in Biblical Theology," in *Conflicts about the Holy Spirit,* ed. Hans Kung and Jürgen Moltmann, trans. G. W. S. Knowles [New York: Seabury, 1979], xiii) reminds us that for Paul, the "peculiarity" or extraordinary manifestation of a "gift" or spiritual experience is not proof of its origin in God's Spirit. "The same phenomena were to be found in paganism (1 Cor. 12:2). All that matters is whether through the gift Christ . . . is recognized as Lord, and the whole community built up." Indeed, the focus on the edification of the body of Christ is so strong that even those who are "prophesying" are instructed to cease talking if another has something to say, "so that all may learn and be encouraged" (1 Cor .14:31). In both cases in 1 Corinthians, διακρίσεις refers to discerning whether a "spiritual utterance" is from God by determining if it confesses Christ's lordship

and edifies the body. In its use outside the Pauline corpus, in Heb. 5:14, διακρίσεις refers to "distinguishing good from evil," a clearly moral category.

In 1 Cor. 2:14–16 ἀνακρίνω and its cognates refer once again to distinguishing the truth of spiritual utterances through the Spirit-formed understanding or through consistency with the Scriptures in Acts 17:11. Indeed the word *gifts* is not in the Greek, in 1 Cor. 12:14. It is better understand πνεύματος τοῦ θεοῦ as the "spiritual things" of God. (See Fee, *First Epistle to the Corinthians,* 118–20. "Spiritual persons" are simply those who have the Spirit.) This passage and 1 Cor. 12–14 are laced with irony. Paul is criticizing the Corinthians, who think they are so very "spiritual" because of the ecstatic issuances in their assembly but who do not practice the genuine mark of spirituality—love as 1 Cor. 13 says.

Very often today, this passage is used in the exact opposite of how Paul intended. It is referenced to talk about a "higher" Christianity of special spiritual knowledge, when Paul actually was referring to discerning the wisdom of the cross vis-à-vis the world. It is meant to express the radically different pattern of living for believers who have the spirit and can, through "spiritual discernment," recognize God's wisdom in the way of the cross. "Being spiritual does not lead to elitism, it leads to a deeper understanding of God's profound mystery—redemption through a crucified messiah" (Fee, *First Epistle to the Corinthians,* 120). Once again, discernment has a distinctly moral intention, for people "with the Spirit" to determine whether instruction or prophecy leads to living out the wisdom of God in the pattern of the cross.

6. Dunn, *Discernment,* 714–17. Dunn describes this as the community fulfilling "the overall obligation of the people of God" ("will of God") because of their "constant inward renewal," by acting according to that which "all people of spiritual and moral sensibility would approve" ("good"), which God would approve ("acceptable"), and that which God's own power will fulfill ("perfect"). The same emphasis is also found in the Johannine literature. See 1 John 4:1–6. Again, the discernment of spirit is based upon consistency with and adherence to the apostolic doctrine of Jesus Christ as God in the flesh.

7. Johnson, *Scripture and Discernment,* 151.

8. Johnson, *Scripture and Discernment,* 124: "It emerges clearly that Paul uses holiness language to describe the character and behavior of the community as a whole, within the understanding of the church as a living temple, the place where the Holy Spirit is present and powerfully active. He uses it, furthermore, not for the cultic actions of the community, but for its moral behavior, which is meant progressively to enact that identity (holiness) which distinguishes this group from those outside it in the world."

9. Two prerequisites for discernment include a prayerful community that is devoted to "apostolic teaching" (Acts 2:42) and a spiritually open community that seeks the Spirit's utterances. In Acts 1:14, we read that before the twelve apostles faced the decision to choose Matthias as an apostle, their fledgling community was already "constantly devoted to prayer." In Acts 4:23–31, when facing the earliest threats of persecution, the church develops a habit of praying corporately for the strength needed to be faithful. (See Johnson, *Scripture and Discernment,* 84.) This pattern is repeated at every place where discernment is needed: *the disciples are committed to prayerful dependence upon God* (see also Acts 6: 6, 11:18, 15:12), *modeling what would become Paul's instruction to the Thessalonians, to "pray without ceasing"* (1 Thess. 5:17). A prayerful community is also a community devoted to the "apostles' teaching" (Acts 2:42). This instruction becomes the first criteria through which all subsequent prophetic words are judged. Both the apostolic witness of the *kerygma* (Jesus is Lord) and tradition (instruction in doctrine) through preaching and teaching provide the context for all further exhortation. (See 1 John 4:1–6. Cf. Johnson, *Scripture and Discernment,* 153.)

For the community devoted to prayer and apostolic teaching, Paul's expectation is that the Spirit will then minister through each person (1 Cor. 12:4–11). While these manifestations of the Spirit will take different forms, the New Testament exhortation is to "strive for the spiritual gifts, especially that you may prophesy" (1 Cor. 14:1). L. T. Johnson (*Scripture and Discernment,* 88) views this prophetic action as coming through both the narratives of preaching and the communal sharing of spiritual experiences for the community's consideration. See also Graham A. Cole ("Religious Experience and Discernment Today," in *Reformed Theological Review* 56:1 [Jan–Apr 1997], 3–5). Cole defines religious experience as "firsthand knowledge of the God of the Scriptures that arises out of life whether accumulated or not." Cole warns of three dangers that all call for communal discernment: (1) overvaluing stories (i.e., "The Christological story is the primary one, not our own. Our stories take their value from the way they resonate with the Christ one"); (2) undervaluing stories (i.e., "We need contemporary stories that resonate with the biblical one"); and (3) inadvertently manufacturing stories (i.e., the desire for spiritual experience tempts us to generate experiences through manipulation).

Of course, not every person or every experience is a narrative for the church to hear. Foremost in consideration was "the character of the prophet," with the church following the Old Testament pattern of listening only to those who "gladly bear the burden of holiness in their lives" (Johnson, *Scripture and Discernment,* 126). Cf. Dunn, "Discernment of the Spirit," 83.

10. Cole, "Religious Experience and Discernment Today," 9, 12. Cole calls *sola scriptura* the *norma normans*, or the "norm that rules the other norms of tradition, reason and experience. . . . Scripture alone is that norm to rule the others."

11. Johnson, *Scripture and Discernment,* 113, 120, 124. See also Cole, "Religious Experience and Discernment Today," 12: "Christians are expected to be a community of character."

12. Chan, *Spiritual Theology,* 220.

13. Didache, 11–13.

Chapter 12

1. Ray S. Anderson, "A Theology for Ministry," in *Theological Foundations for Ministry* (Grand Rapids: Eerdmans, 1979), 20, 7: "Ministry precedes and creates the church," and "ministry is determined and set forth by God's own ministry of revelation and reconciliation in the world."

2. Douglas F. Kelley, "Prayer and Union with Christ," in *Scottish Bulletin of Evangelical Theology* 8:2 (1990), 112.

3. Jacques Ellul, *Prayer and Modern Man*, trans. C. Edward Hopkin (New York: Seabury, 1970), 170.

4. Cf. Donald Bloesch, "Donald Bloesch Responds," in *Evangelical Theology in Transition: Theologians in Dialogue with Donald Bloesch,* ed. Elmer M. Colyer (Downers Grove, Ill.: InterVarsity Press, 1999), 196: "The Spirit works among non-Christian peoples in order to sustain them in the trials of life, yet also to preserve them for a time when they will be confronted and challenged by the redeeming Christ. Common grace is in the service of saving grace."

5. For a discussion of God as the real "seeker" in the world, see Mark D. Roberts, "The Search for God: A Christian Perspective," in Hugh Hewitt, *Searching for God in America* (Dallas: Word, 1996), xix–xviii.

6. For a penetrating, in-depth study of ministry as "embrace" in a world of ethnic and cultural strife, see Miroslav Volf, *Exclusion and Embrace: A Theological Exploration of Identity, Otherness, and Reconciliation* (Nashville: Abingdon, 1996).

7. George C. Hunter, *The Celtic Way of Evangelism* (Nashville: Abingdon, 2000).

8. Volf, *Exclusion and Embrace,* 100.

9. See Ray S. Anderson, *Ministry on the Fireline: A Practical Theology for an Empowered Church* (Downers Grove, Ill.: InterVarsity Press, 1993), 75–76. See also Gordon D. Fee, *The First Epistle to the Corinthians* (Grand Rapids: Eerdmans, 1987), The New International Commentary on the New Testament, 300–301, for a discussion of 1 Cor. 7:14.

10. Volf, *Exclusion and Embrace,* 127: "The very nature of the Triune God is reflected in the cross of Christ."

Conclusion

1. For a provocative study about this and other themes in this book, see William Dyrness, *How America Hears the Gospel* (Grand Rapids: Eerdmans, 1989). In chapter 4, "Virgin Land," Dyrness describes how the "frontier mentality" of early Americans has contributed to a pervasive "pilgrim" motif, as well as a value for the solitary "traveler."

2. Robert Wuthnow, *After Heaven: Spirituality in America since the 1950s* (Berkeley and Los Angeles: University of California Press, 1998), chs. 1 and 2.

3. Wuthnow, *After Heaven,* 168.

4. Wuthnow, *After Heaven*, chs. 3–6.

5. This is a central tenet of Guder et al., *Missional Church* (Grand Rapids: Eerdmans, 1998).

6. John Calvin, *Institutes* 3.1.1.

7. Calvin *Inst.* 3.6.6; 4.17.1: "Our highest perfection is uniformly represented in Scripture as consistency in our conformity and resemblance to God."

8. As Jacob Firet writes, "to be a Christian is to be in the making." To which Firet would quickly add that this "becoming" is best understood as being facilitated by "nurture" (or his more technical term, "agogy"), where human growth and transformation come through the channel of another person, in relationship. See Jacob Firet, *Dynamics of Pastoring* (Grand Rapids: Eerdmans, 1986).

9. Calvin, *Inst.* 1.1.1; 2.2.18.

10. Michael Goldberg, "Discipleship: Basing One Life on Another—It's Not What You Know, It's Who You Know," in Stanley Hauerwas, Nancey Murphy, and Mark Nation, eds. *Theology Without Foundations: Religious Practice and the Future of Theological Truth,* (Nashville: Abingdon Press, 1994), 290–291: "Classically, the students of Jewish Tradition were called *talmidei chachamin*— 'Students of the Wise'— and *not* students of some disembodied, impersonal 'Wisdom.' . . . The knowledge rabbis held out to their communities was decidedly not academic, not essentially a knowing *that* but a knowing *how.* In other words, the tradition which the rabbis both created and transmitted was . . . overarchingly practical."

11. Jürgen Moltmann, *The Church in the Power of the Holy Spirit* (Minneapolis: Fortress, 1993), 220.

12. Ellen T. Charry, "Spiritual Formation by the Doctrine of the Trinity," *Theology Today* 54:3 (October 1997), 372.

13. Charry, "Spiritual Formation," 372.

14. Tom Beaudoin (*Virtual Faith: The Irreverent Spiritual Quest of Generation X* [San Francisco: Jossey-Bass, 1998], 150–51) challenges Gen X seekers to a "wholesale reconsid-

eration of religious tradition" as a means to seeing their "virtual faith" become "authentic lived practice [that is] more truly religious."

15. Charry, "Spiritual Formation," 369.

16. Miroslav Volf, *Exclusion and Embrace: A Theological Exploration of Identity, Otherness, and Reconciliation* (Nashville: Abingdon, 1996), 69–71. Cf. Moltmann, *Trinity and the Kingdom* (1980; repr. Minneapolis: Fortress, 1991), 19.

17. Evangelical theologian Donald Bloesch has recently written that American evangelicalism must confront the individualism that has held sway over the tradition since the Enlightenment. "We must come to see that decision and obedience normally take place in relation to a faith community, leading to vital participation in such a community" (Donald Bloesch, "Donald Bloesch Responds," in *Evangelical Theology in Transition: Theologians in Dialogue with Donald Bloesch*, ed. Elmer M. Colyer [Downers Grove, Ill.: InterVarsity Press, 1999], 207).

Index